CONTEMPORARY PLAYWRIGHTS
ARTHUR MILLER

IN THE SAME SERIES
HAROLD PINTER
SAMUEL BECKETT
JOHN ARDEN
JOHN OSBORNE
ROBERT BOLT
JOHN WHITING
ARNOLD WESKER

CONTEMPORARY PLAYWRIGHTS

ARTHUR MILLER
BY
RONALD HAYMAN

HEINEMANN · LONDON

Heinemann Educational Books Ltd
London Edinburgh Melbourne
Toronto Singapore Auckland
Hong Kong Nairobi
Ibadan Johannesburg

SBN (cased edition)   435 18433 4
SBN (paperback edition) 435 18408 3

Published by Heinemann Educational Books Ltd
48 Charles Street, London W1X 8AH
Printed in Great Britain by
Cox & Wyman Ltd, London, Fakenham and Reading

CONTENTS

264942

ACKNOWLEDGEMENTS

The author and publisher wish to thank the following for permission to reprint copyright material: Arthur Miller and the Cresset Press for extracts from *Death of a Salesman* and *A View from the Bridge;* Arthur Miller and Secker & Warburg for extracts from *All My Sons, A Memory of Two Mondays, The Crucible, After the Fall, Incident at Vichy* and *The Price.*

Part of the interview with Arthur Miller appeared in *The Times* of 15 February 1969 and the author is indebted to the Editor for permission to reprint that part.

The photographs are reproduced by courtesy of Angus McBean.

BIOGRAPHICAL OUTLINE

1915 Born in Harlem, the son of a well-to-do manufacturer who in

1929 lost all his money in the Depression.

1932 Graduated at high school but didn't have the money to go on to college. He started a series of jobs – as a truck-driver, as a crewman on a tanker, as a waiter and then in an automobile parts warehouse at a salary of 15 dollars a week, from which he saved money for university.

1934–8 University of Michigan.

1938 joined the Federal Theatre Project.

1940 married Mary Slattery, whom he had met at college. Rejected by the army on medical grounds, he worked for a year as a fitter in the Brooklyn Navy Yard, at the same time writing plays for radio. He left to write a film script about army training.

1944 Published *Situation Normal*, a report on his experience collecting material for the film.
First Broadway play: *The Man Who Had All the Luck*. But it closed after four performances.

1945 *Focus*, a novel about anti-semitism.

1947 Won the New York Drama Critics' Circle Award for *All My Sons*.

1949 Won the New York Drama Critics' Circle Award, the Pulitzer Prize and the Antoinette Perry Award for *Death of a Salesman*.

1956 Divorced from Mary Slattery and married Marilyn Monroe, summoned to appear before the House Committee for un-American Activities. He refused to co-operate by denouncing his associates and in

Arthur Miller

BIBLIOGRAPHY

Texts

The Cresset Press publish: *Death of a Salesman, A View from the Bridge*.
Secker & Warburg publish: The Collected Plays containing *All My Sons, Death of a Salesman, A Memory of Two Mondays* and *A View from the Bridge* (two-act version).
The Crucible, After the Fall, Incident at Vichy, The Price, I Don't Need You Any More (short stories).
Gollancz publish: *Focus* (novel).
Penguin publish: *The Misfits, A View from the Bridge* and *All My Sons, The Crucible, Death of a Salesman, Incident at Vichy*.
In New York, Viking Press publish all these texts as well as: *Situation Normal* (reportage), *A View from the Bridge* (containing *A Memory of Two Mondays* and the original one-act version of *A View from the Bridge*).

Interviews

The Paris Review No. 38, reprinted in *Writers at Work*, Second Series, Secker & Warburg.
Encounter, July 1959.

Selected Criticism

Dennis Welland, *Arthur Miller*, Writers and Critics, Oliver & Boyd.
Robert Hogan, *Arthur Miller*, University of Minnesota Pamphlets.
Sheila Huftel, *Arthur Miller, The Burning Glass*, W. H. Allen.
Henry Popkin, 'Arthur Miller: The Strange Encounter.'
  Sewanee Review, Winter 1960, reprinted in Alan S. Downer,
  American Drama and Its Critics, Gemini Books, University of Chicago Press.

Arthur Miller

C. W. E. Bigsby, *Confrontation and Commitment, A Study of Contemporary American Drama, 1959–1966,* MacGibbon & Kee.
John Mander, *The Writer and Commitment,* Secker & Warburg.

Performances

November 1944	*The Man Who Had All the Luck,* directed by Joseph Fields at the Forest Theatre, New York
January 1947	*All My Sons* at the Coronet Theatre, New York, directed by Elia Kazan with Ed Begley and Arthur Kennedy
May 1948	*All My Sons* at the Lyric, Hammersmith, directed by Warren Jenkins, with Joseph Calleia and Richard Leech. The production transferred in June to the Globe Theatre
February 1949	*Death of a Salesman* at the Morosco Theatre, New York, directed by Elia Kazan with Lee J. Cobb and Arthur Kennedy
July 1949	*Death of a Salesman* at the Phoenix Theatre, London, with Paul Muni and Kevin McCarthy
December 1950	*An Enemy of the People* (adapted from Henrik Ibsen) at the Broadhurst Theatre, directed by Robert Lewis with Frederick March
January 1953	*The Crucible* at the Martin Beck Theatre directed by Jed Harris with Arthur Kennedy, Beatrice Straight and Madeleine Sherwood
February 1954	*Les Sorcières de Salem* adapted by Marcel Aymé from *The Crucible* at the Théâtre Sarah-Bernhardt, Paris, with Yves Montand, Simone Signoret and Nicole Courcel
November 1954	*The Crucible* at the Bristol Old Vic directed by Warren Jenkins with Edgar Wreford, Rosemary Harris and Pat Sandys
September 1955	*A Memory of Two Mondays* and *A View from the Bridge* (one-act version) at the Coronet Theatre, New York directed by Martin Ritt with Van Heflin and J. Carrol Naish

Bibliography

April 1956	*The Crucible* at the Royal Court Theatre, London, directed by George Devine with Michael Gwynn, Rosalie Crutchley and Mary Ure
October 1956	*A View from the Bridge* (two-act version) at the Comedy Theatre, London, directed by Peter Brook with Anthony Quayle and Michael Gwynn
February 1958	*An Enemy of the People* at the Theatre Royal, Lincoln, directed by John Hale with George Coulouris
September 1958	*A Memory of Two Mondays* at Nottingham Playhouse, directed by Val May with Bryan Pringle and James Cossins
January 1964	*After the Fall* at the Lincoln Centre, New York, directed by Elia Kazan with Jason Robards Jr. and Barbara Loden
December 1964	*Incident at Vichy* at Lincoln Centre, directed by Harold Clurman with David Wayne and Joseph Wiseman
January 1965	*The Crucible* at the Old Vic, London. A National Theatre production directed by Sir Laurence Olivier with Colin Blakely, Joyce Redman and Sarah Miles
January 1966	*Incident at Vichy* at the Phoenix Theatre, London, directed by Peter Wood with Alec Guinness and Anthony Quayle
February 1968	*The Price* at the Morosco Theatre, New York, with Pat Hingle and Arthur Kennedy
March 1969	*The Price* at the Comedy Theatre, London, with Albert Salmi and Shepherd Strudwick (who had taken over from Pat Hingle and Arthur Kennedy in New York)

INTERVIEW

RONALD HAYMAN: *I wanted to ask you about the Willy Lomans we saw in England, Frederick March in the film and Paul Muni on stage as compared with Lee J. Cobb. Who gave you most of what you wanted?*

ARTHUR MILLER: Lee Cobb did it the best from my viewpoint. I felt that – to take the movie first – Freddie March played him as though he were insane. It was a psycho-drama of some sort, and it was not at all his fault; Freddie's a very good actor – he could easily have done it. It was the fault of the director and the screen-writer, who saw the play in totally psychiatric terms – in part I think because they were afraid of the subject matter at that time – the play was very doubtful about American mores and the American system. Actually when they did that play into a movie, Columbia Pictures manufactured a trailer – a short movie on their own to precede the showing of *Death of a Salesman* in all the theatres and that movie was an attempt to extol the trade of salesmanship and to show that in reality and contrary to the movie you were about to see, it was one of the most rewarding professions that a man could follow in this country. It was cultural MacCarthyism and it occurred just about the time the play was being attacked in this country as a time bomb set by Communists to blow up the country. I forbade the showing of the short or trailer and they never showed it. But part of the reason for making Willy seem mad was to take the pressure off what he was talking about.

Paul Muni played it in London and he didn't do it right in the sense that he had come to a time in his career when he was listening to his own voice – he was a very good actor but his style had been superseded twenty years earlier really. The style was too studied, too technical. There was too little real inner life in his performance.

Cobb was the best. As often happens, the man who creates the role originally has the advantage of discovering it all new. And when you discover something in that way you invest yourself in it; you don't protect yourself from it quite the way later people do from the

1

Arthur Miller

performances that preceded them, to do something else even though it may be wrong just to individuate themselves. Cobb was in it, and he of course is personally that way anyway. His nature is superbly fitted for that role.

In some ways The Price *seems to be closer to* All My Sons *and* Death of a Salesman *than any of the intervening plays in the sense that it goes back in a way to the father and two sons relationship even though the father is dead.*

From my point of view, the whole son-father thing is a dried husk in that play. You see it isn't really operative in the way it was in the others. Basically what I was interested in in *The Price* was what it takes to be a person who refuses to be swept away and seduced to the values of the society. It is in one sense the price of integrity. In other words the policeman has refused to adopt the sex and success motives of the society. He has walled himself up against them and he has kept a certain kind of perverse integrity as a result of that but you see what he pays for that. Still, he is saner than Walter, with a hold on reality. So basically what is involved in the forefront of the play is the question of what it takes – the deformations that both viewpoints take in this society. The deformations that are taken on by people who are able somehow to block themselves off from the sweep of opportunity and the never-never land that society promises. The father-son thing is a superficial part of this play, its occasion rather than its subject.

But doesn't the guilt of the father play quite a large part in the pre-history of the play as it does in All My Sons*?*

Yes, but hopefully, you see I wish another writer would have written it, I mean a writer who'd never written of fathers and sons. I purposely leave the father uncharacterized except the misunderstood past, the dead matrix from which the others have sprung. He himself no longer makes any demands, but the sons are struggling with his values in themselves. He is simply there as a shadow really – in fact they neither forgive him nor remember him. He is finally absolved by the others. But it's all now.

2

But Victor is trapped in something that, had he resisted the father more, he could have –

But that is of course so long ago. And he even sees through it himself. The father had diminished in his size – he only has the last laugh, to be sure, as the dead always do because they made us, because they are in us even as we reject them.

I read some critic who said you considered yourself dramaturgically a descendant of Ibsen.

It all comes from one essay I wrote. What I was saying was that you can no more dismiss Ibsen than you can dismiss some kind of architecture that has given birth to other kinds of architecture. He was a strong influence on my early youth but I have no debt to him in the sense that one is insisting upon recreating him all the time. What he gave me in the beginning was a sense of the past and a sense of the rootedness of everything that happens.

How do you feel though about these plays like Pinter's, which almost reject the past altogether in the sense that you never get to know the character's history?

I think of them quite frankly as a kind of naturalism, and by that I mean that in ordinary contact in life you don't ever get very much of somebody's past. You infer and impute things to people but what they're doing is of course in the present. I like his work very much. I can't help wishing, though, that such forcefully built trees would form more tangible fruit.

But a lot of your plays like The Price *could be interpreted in a Freudian way. You can see Victor as conditioned by his father.*

Oh certainly. You see I'm not trying to give an impression of life. I'm trying to analyse something and therefore the past is something you must take into account – it's simply impossible to individuate people in my opinion without it and I don't think we want any past any more in any way. Solomon in *The Price* says it better than I could say it. Nobody wants that kind of furniture because it *implies* a past

3

and it implies that the past can't be broken. They want to go shopping. You see they want a new lease on life, they want to feel they have infinite options, limitless choices. He says there's no more possibilities when you've got furniture like this. You're limited by the past – and of course you are. And it's delusory to think otherwise. I think it's an escape and a romantic one into the bargain. But I'm in a small minority. Most of the art we have is assuming the past isn't there. But I don't think they're dealing most of the time with people, they're dealing with constructs of attitudes to an existence, openly and unabashed. But the past, looked at bravely, can liberate as well as imprison you in repetitions of its illusion.

How important do you think the element of mimicry is in playwriting?

I am a good mimic. I can speak in any dialect I've ever heard. It's very important to me, to know accents and the way people talk, especially in this country where speech and speech mannerisms and habits of language are so deeply connected with attitudes. We have so many different kinds of immigrants, from the Negro to the Swede to the Jew to the Italian. A playwright writes with his ears.

When did you move out of New York?

Not until I went to college, when I was nineteen. Then I went to the Middle West, to Michigan, but up to then I was in New York all the time. I was born in Harlem. I went to grammar school there, and I was part of the time in Brooklyn. But it's the same kind of people basically, except that there were no Negroes in Brooklyn at that time but the other groups were all there. So it's always been part of my life. I was born and brought up in New York City and what somebody was was always connected with what his ethnic background was. I couldn't think except in terms of the differentiation of speech.

I believe you enjoyed writing The Crucible *more than you enjoyed writing any of the other plays. I wonder why you've never gone back to a historical play.*

I might do that again. It was fun because of the fact that I needn't make up the whole story. I didn't do it again I suppose because I never thought of another period that was so relevant to ours and maybe there isn't any. It was a lot of joy – you can just work on the writing. It takes me a year to invent a story. It required an immense amount of sheer editing, you might say. In fact there were hundreds of people involved in this thing as there always are in historical events. I've got five judges in the one judge.

Does it take you longer to invent a story now than it did when you started, because I believe you wrote fourteen or fifteen full length plays before All My Sons.

No I don't think it takes any longer. It took two years for me to write *All My Sons* which has got a very involved story. I don't think that anything has taken me that long to write since.

You used to write in verse – I wonder whether you still do – and then rewrite in prose.

I've done that. I didn't do it on *The Price* because it had no relevancy to that. I've been writing verse for years, but primarily as an exercise, to contract and squeeze the language and clear the mind. So I was never interested in becoming a professional poet. I still do it. But I don't want an audience thinking they're listening to verse because it's beside the point now but I do want them to feel that they're getting a packed, a dense speech without their taking note of the fact that it's at all odd. Maybe I've succeeded too well in fact, because it is one of the criticisms of my work from time to time that it lacks poetry. My attempt has been to make it simply dense, just to advance the action that much more quickly and it's also more pleasurable. I think it's more beautiful that way. Basically what I'm after is the compression of the psychological and social into forward-moving speech with the requisite consciousness. The theatre has to this day never caught up with the consciousness ordinary people have of their social situation. Anyone who goes into a factory and listens to the way people talk, they're way ahead of the theatre, they're so often quite aware that they're right snugly inside a real cul-de-sac in relation to society. You can't talk five minutes with anybody

Arthur Miller

without talking sociology, be he a plumber or a carpenter or anything else. But it is done from his vantage point, with his ignorance and his stupidity and his knowledge. And the compression is purely and simply the compression of his personality and the social attitudes he has without violating his lack of awareness or underrating it.

A good example is Solomon. The ellipses that go into those speeches, the packing of his ... Now of course everybody thinks that it's a great Yiddish accent but in truth the involution of those speeches in which he is relating his own desperation at the age of ninety, trying to decide whether to live or die in effect and the social milieu in which he finds himself – you see it's all webbed together. It is compressed. And I try to do that in everything I can.

Did you find it a problem in A View from the Bridge *moving from the poetic speech of Alfieri to the plain speech of the others?*

Yes I did. You see that story is – to anybody who knows plain Sicilians or Calabrian people – that story is age-old. I didn't know it when I heard it the first time, but just telling it around a few times to people who lived on the waterfront where I used to live, it was quite obvious that – in its details it was a little different but basically the orphan girl or the niece who is not quite a blood relation living in the house is a stick of dynamite which always ends badly and the betrayal by an individual in a passion – his betrayal of some group is part of it, generally. It had myth-like resonance for me. I didn't feel I was making anything up, but rather recording something old and marvellous. I might add that Raf Vallone has toured Italy three times with it and especially in the small southern towns the people, he tells me, react to it almost as a rite.

So in that sense it was a historical play too?

It was. Yeah. I did know a lawyer who worked down on the waterfront – he had nothing to do with this story actually – he'd come from a Neapolitan family and he used to laughingly say 'They're just going through all the Greek myths down here'. Every week somebody comes in and has done or has thought of doing one of the great tragic stories. I sensed a feeling of powerlessness in him; I mean that he'd

6

got to feel that he knew what was going to happen before it happened. And there he was standing just picking up the pieces, and that was the feeling I wanted to get over. So I wanted to lift the language above mere everyday language without giving him too stiff a quality or he couldn't have related to these people. In fact, in life, he did elevate his language with them as he strove for some authority over their passions.

How did you feel about the way it was done in London?

The problem there again for me – you see they couldn't approximate to the dialect. There was just no way to do that, so they made up a dialect of their own but I could never feel at home with it, though the average English audience didn't know the difference. It's probably the way we do a British lord – if you heard it your hair would stand up. But I thought Peter Brook had managed the staging beautifully. His set was quite apt, useful and kind of inevitable. And Quayle did get a sense of the sheer brute gigantic quality of the guy, which is what he'd have to have. And the fellow who played Marco, this Scottish actor —

Ian Bannen

Ian Bannen was terrific in it but it was more related to Scotland basically than it was to Brooklyn. But I think they should do that. They'd have to make a false and tenuous relation to Brooklyn if they were going to do that and that would be less vivid and true than if they made a relation to wherever they came from and whatever they came out of.

But could the production have done more to integrate Alfieri into the action?

Alfieri shouldn't be all that integrated. He is objective, after all. In life, I mean. But perhaps you're right. It was done very simply off-Broadway here – the mixture of contact with Eddie and distance. There was no possibility to disintegrate the relationship because the theatre was only as big as a living-room. When you get up on a big

7

Arthur Miller

stage it's a question of connecting people; when you're on a small stage it's a question of separating them.

I was very interested to see there was a page of typescript of yours in that Paris Review *interview you gave . . .*

That was a weird thing you know. I had been interviewed three or four months earlier than the moment I'm about to tell you of and suddenly they called me up and said, 'Give us anything, something preferably with your handwriting on it.' So I reached in a cabinet where there's a whole pile of undifferentiated paper, perhaps five thousand sheets that go back for twenty years. Maybe five pages of a play I never went on with or twenty pages or it could be two and a half acts that I'd forgotten completely I'd written, and I picked up this lump and there was what seemed to be a fairly amusing page – that is to say one got some feeling out of it. I had no more idea of writing a play with Solomon in it at that time than of writing a play about the Empire State Building, and it was only after the play was opened that somebody mentioned this. It was total accident. I must have started fifty plays in my life that are in that stage.

I took it to be an earlier draft.

Well evidently it was but you see it was a very primitive attempt – I was just sort of playing around on a keyboard with that. I was fooling around with his speech on that page, with the unexpectedness of his speech. Every time he opens his mouth he says not quite what you expected him to say. He's himself, you see, He can't be led anywhere. He appears to be going the way you're going but it turns out he never is. It was a weird coincidence – then a short time after I started to work on *The Price* with that character. I must have been ready to have made that selection but I didn't know it.

How much did you get out of that playwriting course you did at Michigan?

I got probably one most valuable thing – you see when I started out there was no off-Broadway. There was absolutely no place to produce a play except in the commercial theatre, which even then we knew was dying. So one needed an audience and it provided that.

But do you think that playwriting is something that can be taught beyond giving useful criticism of scripts?

It's taught anyway. Nobody who has never been in a theatre or never seen a television show or never seen a movie starts writing plays. It's a conventional form. I don't think you can ever teach anybody to be a playwright who isn't a playwright. Out of that class in Michigan I don't know of another playwright. So that's the answer. But their viewpoint was correct: they said 'It'll make them better audiences.'

Do you think of the size of an audience that you're communicating with?

I don't think of it as such but I can't imagine obliterating the whole thought. I mean the play is so manifestly a communicating mechanism.

But when you were writing The Misfits *and thinking of what must be a mass audience for a film you didn't have to simplify beyond what you would in writing for the stage.*

The reason I'm not a good movie writer and not at home in it is just that. It is wrong of me to do that but I do find myself simplifying. I'm not sure it's that I think the audience is dumber. There's something cruder about the mechanism of the movie – it makes everything – even the so-called philosophical films are strangely banal finally. I suppose it's the fact that words are very much the product of a specific culture and they have ambiguities that are much more subtle than anything you see, it seems to me. Maybe that's why it's so difficult to arrive at a satisfactory dramatic form now, because society is so contradictory that the vocabulary can't socialize experience any more. And images – you believe in it because it's there but that sort of truth is, by itself, rather superficial after all.

Arthur Miller

Would this be tied up with the reason that you're more interested – as you put it yesterday – in analysing rather than in giving an impersonation of life?

I've always done the same thing really in one way or another – and that is to show the process. It's the way my mind works – to ask how something came to be what it is, rather than to play along the apparent surfaces of things to give a sense of what they are . . .

Or to show them in the process of becoming what they are – we see Victor as he has become, we hear about how he has become it.

The same thing with Willy Loman or anyone else in my plays. And that's a foregone or a foresworn aim now, it appears to me. It's probably because so many theories of how one becomes anything are so exploded now. But it's also I think that nobody really wants to be positioned as being responsible for what he's doing and if you invoke that idea it's very dubious to people if only because it implies that they must and can make choices and exercise will.

Are you interested in this Hippy movement as a playwright? You use a policeman who is a drop-out from society but you haven't handled any young characters in the recent plays.

Actually I've been fooling with an original film script in which the leading character might be called hip.

You made a remark about a playwright needing special knowledge of a subject.

Yeah, I think that in the little area in which he works he ought to be or to feel he is the expert. I think he should have special knowledge. Otherwise it becomes derivative – I think that's the problem now. A lot of these people there are deriving their impressions from the other person: there's a great mythology now as to what – for example you mentioned the Hippies – as to what they are, what they're about and who they are. And there's a curious thing about it – you can never really find one, they're always referring to somebody else. One almost believes it's a figment of advertising, a lot of

10

people chasing a mode. If you approach somebody as a hippy you are going to get nowhere, because after all he is a citizen and a person, far less certain than the mode would have him, far more susceptible of pain. That's why I think even in all the years that have gone by since the Hippy thing started and with all the writers who are involved in it, no Hippy qua Hippy has popped up in a work in a convincing way as a human being. It's a strange thing. You would think that somebody would have come along with the Willy Loman of the Hippies, the archetype. And I have a feeling that it's because so much of the attitude that is called Hippy is so outer-related – it's so much a self-conscious thing that it has no reverberations, it has no depth – they are never seen as private people, always as examples.

But there's a sort of movement of fashion now isn't there against the idea of the possibility of being wholly known – you use that phrase about Eddie Carbone. In a sense all your central characters need to become wholly known.

It's quite the opposite now – the need now is to become a more or less distinct possibility but by no means become wholly known because it must be false – it would contradict the unpredictability of life. The whole idea of process is out of the window – it is gone – it's unstylish, it's unfashionable because nothing has happened as it should have, supposedly. And my reaction to it is that it simply means that the capacity for sensing reality has been defective and one must develop better sensory apparatus to find out what's going on, rather than relapsing into a kind of self-satisfied feeling that since everything is unpredictable, to hell with it and live for tomorrow morning and so on. That kind of demoralization was always present, though; it simply lacked a triumphant stylishness.

Would I be right in thinking that for you the process of writing After the Fall *was some such experience of thinking your way through a patch of experience in which you had to put yourself into a play in a different way from which you ever did before?*

Yeah, well it's an attempt to find some viable synthesis of the experience instead of simply roaming around in the experience, which leaves the experience where it was you know, to try to render the chaos and at the same time to seek out whatever structure it has. *The Price* goes in the other direction more – it emphasizes the structuring of experience because it is a play about the impact of the past but there are endless possibilities which I don't think I've reached yet in the direction of doing two things at the same time. I suppose by structure I always mean the same thing which is a paradox – that's the existence of fate, or high probability, which means that when a man starts out to do what he intends to do, he creates forces which he never bargained for, but whose contradictions nevertheless spring dialectically from the force of his thrust. I think this is true of almost every play. And then he's got to relate himself to what the results of his actions were. It's true of Eddie Carbone, it's true of Willy Loman, it's true of John Proctor. What I find myself trying to face more and more openly is the existence of human will as an ultimate category. I tried to do it in *After the Fall* – I mean at the end of the play he has to decide that it is at least equally real that when he wakes up in the morning, he feels like a boy, he feels wonderful in spite of all this and that that sense of life and promise is also possibly valid . . . In other words to choose to use that energy which is the energy towards life as opposed to simply giving way to the desolation of what he knows to be the result of experience. For the latter is a cancelling-out of the life force that he knows he feels alongside of despair. A decision has to be made. And in *The Price* a man is faced with the fact that he participated in his own alienation from himself and in so doing discovers himself in what he did. In short, a far higher consciousness of our own powers over life still awaits us as a breed. I might add that in this lies a real revolution. Victor Franz refuses to merely rediscover the love he put into the house and finally persists in seeing it as a value, whatever others made of it.

But doesn't the play in a sense act as his accomplice in exculpating him – I mean the guilt of the father, from the way it's brought in in the second act, does seem to be an explanation of what's happened, as though Dad is responsible?

Except that ultimately as it turns out he knew that the old man had something. So it's split. I can't say – I don't think anybody can – that it was all him or all so to speak the society or the past. But there's a point comes where one has to move, with insufficient evidence, always.

But does this work for you as completely as you'd like it to? I think it succeeds in large measure but what I can't a hundred per cent accept is the relationship which you establish very forcibly at the beginning of the play about the impossibility of living according to the ideal and then the narrowing of the focus to these personal relationships in which the family doesn't seem to be entirely effective as an incarnation of Society for the play's purposes.

It works to this degree and that is that ultimately the mystery remains as to where the decisive spring is, and I like that about it. It's open, I've tried as far as I could to set forth the balance of evidence and I don't know how else you can set forth an organism otherwise – excepting in some extreme situations which by their extremity are not interesting. I guess the impulse I had was more to open up a life and its process than to lay judgement, in the sense that the two forces were laid bare to the point where the man could recognize himself in his own actions. When this play starts he says 'I can't find myself in what I've done' – until he discovers again that he did love the old man; it's the recrudescence of that feeling that illuminates for him how he got into this – so that his experience becomes his own then rather than some imposed unreality. That is the story structure of the thing to me – the web of social and individual impulses which form a fate.

One of the things I like very much about it is that it doesn't take him to any extreme action as your early central characters have often had to be carried to in order to expose themselves.

Yeah well that's a limitation as well in my sense of the reality of this kind of a man. He couldn't have done what he did with the discipline with which he did it and then suddenly break with the whole character that he's got. This too is unacceptable today. You see it implies that people have limits. What we're presented with all the time is somebody suddenly doing something which is absolutely inexplicable by any standards for the theatrical effect. And it is easier to do that because, again, nobody on the stage has a past any more.

In a sense After the Fall *is the play in which you've come most directly to grips with this kind of battle against disintegration and it was a great pity that the reactions to it was obviously so utterly different from what you'd expected.*

They never dealt with the play in any way, shape or fashion. There's a threatening idea in it. What it's saying in effect is that choice is still there, necessary and implicit and that the disaster is there and that you choose to hope because you are alive and don't commit suicide, which implies a certain illusionism and so forth but the only hope there is nevertheless.

Incident at Vichy was written as a companion piece. Even when one doesn't know what one has done, finally the responsibility for it can only rest with oneself. But the character who reacts with conscientiousness is the most unalienated on the stage. He's the only one who's approachable.

But the style is so different from After the Fall.

It is the structure of the dilemma, the structure unabashed. I wanted to deal more objectively with experience. There's a certain amount of alienation in the way it's presented, in the way people stand up and say what they are. It's rather in a Molière tradition. A man gets up and tells you pretty much what he's about; the only question is what meaning the conflict will arrive at. There are types, there are kinds of people who act severely within the limits of their types and most of the people on stage are like that in this play.

But the action isn't inside the head.

It's the play most related to *Death of a Salesman*. I have worked in two veins always and I guess they alternate. In one the event is inside the brain and in the other the brain is inside the event. In *Death of a Salesman* we are inside the head. That's why I've needed two kinds of stylistic attack.

14

ALL MY SONS

When *All My Sons* is praised, it is usually praised rather disparagingly – a well-made play but a good one. Then something is usually said about Miller's debt to Ibsen.

In performance, what is most immediately striking is the naturalness of the backyard life – the leisureliness of family life on a Sunday morning, the slightly strained cameraderie of the exchanges of weak wisecracks with the neighbours, the intra-family plotting, the inconsequential mood changes and the movement of the conversation in an illogical series of semi-circles and tangents, which is as much Chekhovian as Ibsenian. Miller's deftness of touch in rendering the flavour of provincial life is also reminiscent of Chekhov.

It is Ibsenian, of course, as Miller has himself said in the Introduction to his Collected Plays, in the sense that the story is nearly over before the action starts. Much of the time has therefore to be spent in bringing the past into the present. But what is remarkable is how neatly Miller does this, and it is worth analysing the construction in some detail.

We notice the broken apple tree the moment the lights came up but Joe Keller is half-way through his conversation with his neighbour Frank before they talk about last night's storm which blew it down. Even the tree has been called an Ibsenian symbol but its main function is to introduce the plot as it does when Frank talks about it as 'Larry's tree' and mentions that he is working on Larry's horoscope. After this it is easy for Miller to start planting the play's prehistory. Joe's son Larry, a pilot, was reported missing during the war, three years ago, and Kate, his mother, still refuses to believe that he is dead.

Another neighbour, Dr Jim Bayliss, and his overweight wife, Sue, who never lets him out of her sight for longer than she can help, let us know that there is a beautiful girl in the house. Ann, who was Larry's fiancée, is staying with the Kellers at the invitation of Chris, the younger son and we learn from Frank's wife, Lydia, that they are living in the house which used to belong to Ann's father.

Arthur Miller

But we do not get any more of the plot yet. First we have a lot of banter. After Chris, who wants to read the book-section of the Sunday paper, has teased his father about his ignorance, we see Joe rather charmingly playing policemen with Jim's young son, kidding the boy into believing that there is a jail inside the house. It is only then that Chris, who wants to marry Ann, tries to get his father to side with him in the fight this is bound to involve with Kate, who still thinks of Ann as Larry's fiancée. We also get our first focus on two very important points: the closeness of the relationship between Joe and Chris, and the difference between their attitudes to the family business.

CHRIS: I'd hoped that if I waited, Mother would forget Larry and then we'd have a regular wedding and everything happy. But if that can't happen here, then I'll have to get out.

KELLER: What the hell is *this?*

CHRIS: I'll get out. I'll get married and live some place else. Maybe in New York.

KELLER: Are you crazy?

CHRIS: I've been a good son too long, a good sucker. I'm through with it.

KELLER: You've got a business here, what the hell is this?

CHRIS: The business! The business doesn't inspire me.

KELLER: Must you be inspired?

CHRIS: Yes. I like it an hour a day. If I have to grub for money all day long at least at evening I want it beautiful. I want a family, I want some kids, I want to build something I can give myself to. Annie is in the middle of that. Now . . . where do I find it?

KELLER: You mean – [*Goes to him*] Tell me something, you mean you'd leave the business?

CHRIS: Yes. On this I would.

KELLER [*after a pause*]: Well . . . you don't want to think like that.

CHRIS: Then help me stay here.

KELLER: All right, but – but don't think like that. Because what the hell did I work for? That's only for you, Chris, the whole shootin' match is for you!

CHRIS: I know that, Dad. Just you help me stay here.

Kate's appearance immediately shows how hard the fight is going to be. In the earlier drafts of the play she was the dominant character and there was a great stress on her belief in astrology. Though Miller later shifted the main focus to the father-son relationship, Kate remains a dominating personality and she has the first speech in which the language rises above the pedestrian level of chat, argument and wisecracks. There is a lyrical rhetoric in her description of the dream from which she awoke to see the tree break and the mercury in Chris's rhetorical thermometer jumps in response.

MOTHER: I was fast asleep, and – [*Raising her arm over the audience.*] Remember the way he used to fly low past the house when he was in training? When we used to see his face in the cockpit going by? That's the way I saw him. Only high up. Way, way up, where the clouds are. He was so real I could reach out and touch him. And suddenly he started to fall. And crying, crying to me . . . Mom, Mom! I could hear him like he was in the room. Mom! . . . it was his voice! If I could touch him I knew I could stop him, if I could only – [*Breaks off, allowing her outstretched hand to fall.*] I woke up and it was so funny – The wind . . . it was like the roaring of his engine. I came out here . . . I must've still been half asleep. I could hear that roaring like he was going by. The tree snapped right in front of me – and I like – came awake. [*She is looking at tree. She suddenly realizes something, turns with a reprimanding finger shaking slightly at* KELLER.] See? We should never have planted that tree. I said so in the first place; it was too soon to plant a tree for him.

CHRIS [*alarmed*]: Too soon!

MOTHER [*angering*]: We rushed into it. Everybody was in such a hurry to bury him. I *said* not to plant it yet. [*To* KELLER] I *told* you to –!

CHRIS: Mother, Mother! [*She looks into his face.*] The wind blew it down. What significance has that got? What are you talking about? Mother, please . . . don't go through it all again, will you? It's no good, it doesn't accomplish anything. I've been thinking, y'know? – maybe we ought to put our minds to forgetting him?

MOTHER: That's the third time you've said that this week.

CHRIS: Because it's not right; we never took up our lives again.

Arthur Miller

We're like at a railroad station waiting for a train that never comes in.

MOTHER [*pressing top of her head*]: Get me an aspirin, heh?

Again, when she is left alone with Joe, the rhythm in Kate's speeches and the slight but significant deviations from natural conversational syntax give Kate a formidable impressiveness. Her stupidity and her stubborn superstitiousness come almost to seem like a dignified refusal to be bound by the norms of reasonableness.

When Jim's young son comes back, she gets very worked up about the jail game Joe is playing with him.

MOTHER: Go home, Bert. [BERT *turns around and goes up driveway. She is shaken. Her speech is bitten off, extremely urgent.*] I want you to stop that, Joe. That whole jail business!

KELLER [*alarmed, therefore angered*]: Look at you, look at you shaking.

MOTHER [*trying to control herself, moving about clasping her hands*]: I can't help it.

KELLER: What have I got to hide? What the hell is the matter with you, Kate?

MOTHER: I didn't say you had anything to hide, I'm just telling you to stop it! Now stop it!

But almost before his denial can make the suspicion dawn in our minds that maybe he has got something to hide, Ann has come out on the porch and good-natured banter is resumed. Until, rather mystifyingly, the theme of her father is introduced.

MOTHER: Your mother – she's not getting a divorce, heh?

ANN: No, she's calmed down about it now. I think when he gets out they'll probably live together. In New York, of course.

MOTHER: That's fine, Because your father is still – I mean he's a decent man after all is said and done.

ANN: I don't care. She can take him back if she likes.

The conversation switches to Larry and Ann denies that she is waiting for him. It is when the tactless Frank comes on that we find out Steve, her father, is in prison.

FRANK [*Funereally*]: And your dad? Is he –?

ANN [*abruptly*]: Fine. I'll be in to see Lydia.

18

FRANK [*sympathetically*]: How about it, does Dad expect a
parole soon?

ANN [*with growing ill-ease*]: I really don't know, I –

FRANK [*staunchly defending her father for her sake*]: I mean
because I feel, y'know, that if an intelligent man like your
father is put in prison, there ought to be a law that says either
you execute him, or let him go after a year.

CHRIS [*interrupting*]: Want a hand with that ladder, Frank?

We now see how cleverly Miller has prepared the ground for this
revelation with the game about the jail and Kate's reaction to it.
The ensuing conversation makes it clear that Joe was in partnership
with Steve and narrowly escaped going to prison himself after they
had sold cracked cylinder heads to the Army Air Force, causing
twenty-one planes to crash in Australia.

As C. W. E. Bigsby has pointed out in his book *Confrontation and
Commitment**, the plot here bears some resemblance to Ibsen's in *The
Wild Duck*, in which one of two business partners is found guilty of
fraud while the other goes free. And like Ibsen's Gregers Werle, Chris
is an idealist who later on, when he finds out about his father's guilt,
feels compelled to destroy the lie on which his father's life is based,
at whatever cost. All we know now though is that Ann, who thinks
her father is the guilty one, does not allow herself to pity him or go on
loving him.

ANN: You're the only one I know who loves his parents.

CHRIS: I know. It went out of style, didn't it?

ANN [*with a sudden touch of sadness*]: It's all right. It's a good
thing.

Joe, on the other hand, believes that family loyalty should have
priority over everything else.

Except for *The Crucible* and *Incident at Vichy*, every major play of
Miller's has featured love and hate between the grown-up child and
the parent.† Even in *A View from the Bridge*, Eddie is virtually a

* MacGibbon & Kee.

† In 'The Shadows of the Gods', a lecture he gave before the New Dramatists
Committee and published in Harper's, Miller pointed to the moment of revolt
against the parent as the starting point of individual development. 'We are
formed in this world when we are sons and daughters and the first truths we
know throw us into conflict with our fathers and mothers.'

Arthur Miller

father to Catherine. In *All My Sons*, the love between the generations is both more prominent and more convincing than the love between Chris and Ann, which is rather tamely written, or than Chris's love for the soldiers who served under him in the war, which is rather over-written.

> CHRIS: Because they weren't just men. For instance, one time it'd been raining several days and this kid came to me, and gave me his last pair of dry socks. Put them in my pocket. That's only a little thing – but ... that's the kind of guys I had. They didn't die; they killed themselves for each other. I mean that exactly; a little more selfish and they'd've been here today. And I got an idea – watching them go down. Everything was being destroyed, see, but it seemed to me that one new thing was made. A kind of – responsibility. Man for man. You understand me? – To show that, to bring that on to the earth again like some kind of a monument and everyone would feel it standing there, behind him, and it would make a difference to him. [*Pause.*] And then I came home and it was incredible. I – there was no meaning in it here; the whole thing to them was a kind of a – bus accident. I went to work with Dad, and that rat-race again. I felt – what you said – ashamed somehow. Because nobody was changed at all. It seemed to make suckers out of a lot of guys. I felt wrong to be alive, to open the bank-book, to drive the new car, to see the new refrigerator. I mean you can take those things out of a war, but when you drive that car you've got to know that it came out of the love a man can have for a man, you've got to be a little better because of that. Otherwise what you have is really loot, and there's blood on it.

This is too obviously a direct statement of something Miller felt. He felt it deeply and sincerely but the sentiment, though certainly relevant to the drama, is not sufficiently dramatized.

The action, however, moves quickly onwards. All seems to be going well between Chris and Ann, but her brother George, a lawyer, who has never before visited their father in prison, has been there today and is now on the telephone to say that he is on his way over. Ann goes in to speak to him and Joe's nervousness reminds us of his 'What have I got to hide?' Kate obviously shares his anxiety and the

act ends on a note of suspenseful foreboding when she warns him that
he will now have to be smart.

The bitchy Sue is well used at the beginning of Act Two. After a
superficially friendly chat with Ann she asks her not to settle down
with Chris in the neighbourhood because of the effect he has on her
husband.

SUE: Jim's a successful doctor. But he's got an idea he'd like to
do medical research. Discover things. You see?

ANN: Well, isn't that good?

SUE: Research pays twenty-five dollars a week minus laundering
the hair-shirt. You've got to give up your life to go into it.

ANN: How does Chris –

SUE [*with growing feeling*]: Chris makes people want to be better
than it's possible to be. He does that to people.

And towards the end of the conversation she contributes usefully
towards the build-up to the *scène à faire* to come when she throws
away the line:

Everybody knows Joe pulled a fast-one to get out of jail.

When Chris comes out, Ann passes on the doubt about Joe and
when Joe comes out, after some pleasant ragging, he increases our
suspicions by offering Ann to set George up with some friends of his
in a local legal practice and to help Steve by taking him back into the
business when he comes out of prison. When Chris objects, the tension mounts, only to be relaxed immediately when the gentle Lydia
comes on to help arrange Kate's hair for the party they are planning
for the evening. But it is pulled sharply taut again when Jim, who
has driven George from the station, rushes in to warn the others not
to let him in, saying that Kate is in no fit state to have this 'exploded
in front of her'.

George comes in under his own steam and ominously recoils from
physical contact with Chris and with Ann. The storm seems about to
break when Ann notices he is wearing a hat.

GEORGE: Your father's – He asked me to wear it.

ANN: How is he?

GEORGE: He got smaller.

ANN: Smaller?

GEORGE: Yeah, little. [*Holds out his hand to measure.*] He's a little man. That's what happens to suckers, you know. It's good I went to him in time – another year there'd be nothing left but his smell.

Peremptorily George tells her she is not going to marry Chris. Ann tries to soothe him but he bursts out with the story. On the crucial day, Joe had stayed at home pretending to be sick and given Steve instructions over the telephone to cover over the cracks in the cylinder heads.

When Kate comes out, all is sweetness again on the surface while underneath it the question of whether Ann and Chris believe George's story remains unanswered. George responds readily to Kate's warmth, and the reappearance of Lydia – all four neighbours are very adroitly exploited – reminds him painfully of the chance of marrying her that he has missed. Kate shows her solidarity with Joe in preparing the ground for the bribe he has up his sleeve for George and she even adds a bribe of her own: she will find a girl for him. The banter this provokes makes a fizzing cocktail mixture with the tension.

When Joe comes out, he is strained but George is gentle. It seems quite possible he will not force a showdown and he may even submit to their concerted wooing of him. It is a casual remark of Joe's about never having had a day's sickness in his life which seems about to precipitate a climax. But it is averted by Frank's untimely entrance with Larry's horoscope. And when he goes, it becomes a different climax from the one we expect. Kate tries to make Ann leave with George. She flatly refuses unless Chris tells her to go. Chris only tells George to go and when Ann supports Chris, George meekly obeys, perhaps a little implausibly after his earlier show of ferocious indignation.

It is through Kate that Miller tries to weld the two themes together:

MOTHER: Your brother's alive, darling, because if he's dead your father killed him. Do you understand me now? As long as you live, that boy is alive. God does not let a son be killed by his father. Now you see, don't you? Now you see.

And when Chris confronts Joe with a direct accusation, his apologia merges the business ethic of survival into his love for his son:

KELLER: You're a boy, what could I do! I'm in business, a man is in business; a hundred and twenty cracked, you're out of business; you got a process, the process don't work you're out of business; you don't know how to operate, your staff is no good; they close you up, they tear up your contracts, what the hell's it to them? You lay forty years into a business and they knock you out in five minutes, what could I do, let them take forty years, let them take my life away? [*His voice cracking.*] I never thought they'd install them. I swear to God. I thought they'd stop 'em before anybody took off.

CHRIS: Then why'd you ship them out?

KELLER: By the time they could spot them I thought I'd have the process going again, and I could show them they needed me and they'd let it go by. But weeks passed and I got no kick-back, so I was going to tell them.

CHRIS: Then why didn't you tell them?

KELLER: It was too late. The paper, it was all over the front page, twenty-one went down, it was too late. They came with handcuffs into the shop, what could I do? [*He sits on bench*] Chris ... Chris, I did it for you, it was a chance and I took it for you. I'm sixty-one years old, when would I have another chance to make something for you? Sixty-one years old you don't get another chance, do ya?

Chris's passionate retort makes an effective curtain, but the rhetorical language is something of a let-down.

CHRIS [*with burning fury*]: For me! Where do you live, where have you come from? For me! – I was dying every day and you were killing my boys and you did it for me? What the hell do you think I was thinking of, the goddam business? Is that as far as your mind can see, the business? What is that, the world – the business? What the hell do you mean, you did it for me? Don't you have a country? Don't you live in the world? What the hell are you? You're not even an animal, no animal kills his own, what are you? What must I do to you? I ought to tear the tongue out of your mouth, what must I do? [*With his fist he pounds down upon his father's shoulder. He stumbles away, covering his face as he weeps.*] What must I do, Jesus God, what must I do?

KELLER: Chris ... My Chris ...

Arthur Miller

Again at the beginning of Act Three, the neighbours are skilfully used. It is two o'clock in the morning and Jim comes in from an emergency operation to find Kate still rocking in her chair on the porch waiting for Chris. Again the language is disappointing as Jim tries to reassure her.

> JIM: Oh, no, he'll come back. We all come back, Kate. These private little revolutions always die. The compromise is always made. In a peculiar way, Frank is right – every man does have a star. The star of one's honesty. And you spend your life groping for it, but once it's out it never lights again. I don't think he went very far. He probably just wanted to be alone to watch his star go out.

The simplicity of Joe's language when he talks about the family is much more acceptable. It is what we expect from him.

> KELLER: There's nothin' he could do that I wouldn't forgive. Because he's my son. Because I'm his father and he's my son.
> MOTHER: Joe, I tell you –
> KELLER: Nothin's bigger than that. And you're goin' to tell him, you understand? I'm his father and he's my son, and if there's something bigger than that I'll put a bullet in my head!

Altogether, the situation is far more brilliantly contrived than the speeches and Ann is given two excellent trumps. First she offers to keep silent about Joe if Kate will agree to her marriage with Chris, and when Kate's stubbornness proves stronger even than her concern for her husband, Ann plays her ace – Larry's letter. Kate moans as she reads it but it is not read out loud until after Chris has come back, intending to go away on his own.

> CHRIS: I could jail him! I could jail him, if I were human any more. But I'm like everybody else now. I'm practical now. You made me practical.
> MOTHER: But you have to be.
> CHRIS: The cats in that alley are practical, the bums who ran away when we were fighting were practical. Only the dead ones weren't practical. But now I'm practical, and I spit on myself. I'm going away. I'm going now.
> ANN [going up to him]: I'm coming with you.

CHRIS: No, Ann.

ANN: Chris, I don't ask you to do anything about Joe.

CHRIS: You do, you do.

ANN: I swear I never will.

CHRIS: In your heart you always will.

ANN: Then do what you have to do!

CHRIS: Do what? What is there to do? I've looked all night for a reason to make him suffer.

ANN: There's reason, there's reason!

CHRIS: What? Do I raise the dead when I put him behind bars? Then what'll I do it for? We used to shoot a man who acted like a dog, but honour was real there, you were protecting something. But here? This is the land of the great big dogs, you don't love a man here, you eat him! That's the principle; the only one we live by – it just happened to kill a few people this time, that's all. The world's that way, how can I take it out on him? What sense does that make? This is a zoo, a zoo!

Again the language is too banal and flat to reach the level of intensity required by the situation. The situation carries it theatrically but it does not justify the way Chris accepts Joe's attempt to shift the blame on to the capitalist system. Chris is much too much of an idealist, a lover of mankind to agree, even in this mood, that Joe is no worse than most men.

KELLER: Who worked for nothin' in that war? When they work for nothin', I'll work for nothin'. Did they ship a gun or a truck outa Detroit before they got their price? Is that clean? It's dollars and cents, nickels and dimes; war and peace, it's nickels and dimes, what's clean? Half the goddam country is gotta go if I go! That's why you can't tell me.

CHRIS: That's exactly why.

KELLER: Then ... why am *I* bad?

CHRIS: *I* know you're no worse than most men but I thought you were better. I never saw you as a man. I saw you as my father.

The theme of filial love is blurring the moral focus. It is the moral condemnation from his other son, who crashed his plane out of shame, that drives Joe to a change of heart. He says he will give himself up to the police.

Arthur Miller

> MOTHER: You're so foolish. Larry was your son too, wasn't he?
> You know he'd never tell you to do this.
> KELLER [*looking at letter in his hand*]: Then what is this if it isn't
> telling me? Sure, he was my son. But I think to him they were
> all my sons. And I guess they were, I guess they were. I'll be
> right down. [*Exits into house.*]

Once inside the house he shoots himself, which produces a highly
theatrical curtain without making the change of heart theatrically
valid. It is always hard to dramatize a profound inner change in a
play in which plot and situation are contrived as tightly as they are
here – unless the language is poetic. Which is not, of course, to say
that it needs to be written in verse. Ibsen, Strindberg and Chekhov
all filtered poetry from the situation into prose dialogue. And in *Death
of a Salesman* so did Arthur Miller.

DEATH OF A SALESMAN

Death of a Salesman is I think, the best American play ever written. It may be more demonstrably flawed than its closest rivals (*Who's Afraid of Virginia Woolf* and the best of Tennessee Williams) but it is a much richer play, with more range and more resonance. It is also more of a public play and probably the only successful twentieth-century tragedy with an unheroic hero.

Willy Loman's values are very much those of contemporary society – the American Dream which the rest of the world mimics – and his downfall derives both from his personal failure in relation to his values and from the failure of the values themselves. Far more than Elmer Rice's Mr Zero or any other modern Everyman, Willy Loman articulates through the way he lives and dies the latent self-destructiveness of a society in which the false promises of advertising corrode not only our business lives but our personal relationships. His only hubris is in believing the propaganda of a success-oriented society. The promises he makes to himself, to Linda, his wife, and to Biff and Happy, his sons, are equally hollow. Nothing is more important to him than his family but his main idea in bringing up his sons is to teach them to cash in on their personal attractiveness – to equip them, in effect, for successful careers in selling. Living in an atmosphere of sales-talk, and making his livelihood out of sales-talk, he can no longer think in any other terms.

In both technique and subject-matter, *Death of a Salesman* owes a lot to the Expressionist drama of the thirties but it digests everything that it borrows and Willy is no anonymous cipher. Miller may see him as a prototype and portmanteau his name out of 'low man' but he also empathizes deeply enough to endow him with a forceful individuality. In writing, as he tells us in the Introduction to his Collected Plays, he made the assumption 'that everyone knew Willy Loman'. We do, but Miller does not therefore try to take short cuts in characterizing him.

Again he starts his story near the end. Willy is already on the point of cracking up when the action starts. But instead of pipelining the

27

past into the present through conversation, Miller resurrects it in action. It is Willy's state of mind which makes this possible.

> He is literally at that terrible moment when the voice of the past is no longer distant but quite as loud as the voice of the present.... There are no flashbacks in this play but only a mobile concurrency of past and present, and this, again, because in his desperation to justify his life Willy Loman has destroyed the boundaries between now and then, just as anyone would do who on picking up his telephone, discovered that this perfectly harmless act had somehow set off an explosion in his basement. The previously assumed and believed-in results of ordinary and accepted actions, and their abrupt and unforeseen – but apparently logical – effects, form the basic collision in this play, and I suppose, its ultimate irony.

Originally the play was conceived as a monodrama and the original title was *The Inside of His Head*. Later Miller found it was better to present parts of the action from other viewpoints than Willy's but for most of the time, when Willy remembers something, we see it as if it were happening here and now. The medium enters into the madness. It is only at the beginning that we are able to feel detached from him and to look down on him pityingly as an anxiety-ridden old man who mumbles to himself in the kitchen or when we hear him talking to Linda and getting confused about whether he has just been driving his Studebaker or the Chevrolet he had in 1928. But when his two sons (whom we have already seen in the present tense) bound on to the stage looking much younger, we know we are watching what Willy is remembering.

Obviously a man with Willy's capacity for self-deception would have a memory which not only selects but distorts. How much his memory is editing the past is something the play cannot tell us. But this is less of a disadvantage than might be expected. Willy is every bit as son-fixated as Joe Keller, and while the boys are young, nearly all his hopes are pinned on their future. Besides illuminating the falseness of the promises he has made both to them and to himself about them, the constant shifts between past and present show us the consequences of his indulgent treatment of them. He has encouraged their weaknesses and inflated their image of themselves so high that when they grow up, it is an unforgivable and almost intolerable let-down to find that being personable and being good at sports is not enough to ensure financial security and popularity in the adult world.

So the problem of integrating themes no longer arises in the same way that it did in *All My Sons*. It is still there, of course, but it is subordinate to the problem of controlling the interflow of tenses. This Miller solves very well indeed, without once leaving us in any doubt about whether we are in the past or the present. And he manages without any cumbersome set-changes. The home is there, aptly, in the background throughout the action. Variations are provided simply by using changes of costume, props, different lighting effects, different areas of the bare forestage. The fluidity Miller contrives is such that he can sometimes make great capital out of the speed at which Willy's mind oscillates between past and present. An example is the scene with the neighbour Charley when Willy's dead brother Ben appears to him and he is conversing partly with the real man, partly with the image in his mind.

WILLY: I'm getting awfully tired, Ben.
　　　[BEN'S *music is heard.* BEN *looks around at everything.*]
CHARLEY: Good, keep playing; you'll sleep better. Did you call me Ben?
　　　[BEN *looks at his watch.*]
WILLY: That's funny. For a second there you reminded me of my brother Ben.
BEN: I only have a few minutes. [*He strolls, inspecting the place.* WILLY *and* CHARLEY *continue playing.*]
CHARLEY: You never heard from him again, heh? Since that time?
WILLY: Didn't Linda tell you? Couple of weeks ago we got a letter from his wife in Africa. He died.
CHARLEY: That so.
BEN [*chuckling*]: So this is Brooklyn, eh?
CHARLEY: Maybe you're in for some of his money.
WILLY: Naa, he had seven sons. There's just one opportunity I had with that man . . .
BEN: I must make a train, William. There are several properties I'm looking at in Alaska.

WILLY: Sure, sure! If I'd gone with him to Alaska that time, everything would've been totally different.

CHARLEY: Go on, you'd froze to death up there.

WILLY: What're you talking about?

BEN: Opportunity is tremendous in Alaska, William. Surprised you're not up there.

WILLY: Sure, tremendous.

CHARLEY: Heh?

WILLY: There was the only man I ever met who knew the answers.

CHARLEY: Who?

BEN: How are you all?

WILLY [taking a pot, smiling]: Fine, fine.

CHARLEY: Pretty sharp tonight.

BEN: Is Mother living with you?

WILLY: No, she died a long time ago.

CHARLEY: Who?

By now we are quite prepared for this sort of thing to happen. At the beginning of the play the scene between Biff and Happy in the bedroom is intercut with the scene between Willy and Linda in the kitchen. Both give us plenty of pointers to Willy's state of near-breakdown. He has come back early from a journey, finding that he cannot keep his mind on his driving. He talks of admiring the country scenery on the road and he talks nostalgically of the time when the neighbourhood was less built-up, when there were less cars and more trees on the street. So from the start, the claustrophobia of the present is linked with mechanization and urbanization, and the madness is linked with a nostalgia for the better times in the past. But though Willy talks longingly of nature, the country, the open-air life, he calls Biff a lazy bum for thinking that he is more likely to 'find himself' – a favourite phrase of Miller's – by working on a farm than he is by working in business. We soon come to expect Willy's opinions and feelings to be self-contradictory. He even contradicts himself verbally within a matter of five speeches.

WILLY: Biff is a lazy bum!

LINDA: They're sleeping. Get something to eat. Go on down.

WILLY: Why did he come home? I would like to know what brought him home.

LINDA: I don't know. I think he's still lost, Willy. I think he's very lost.

WILLY: Biff Loman is lost. In the greatest country in the world a young man with such – personal attractiveness, gets lost. And such a hard worker. There's one thing about Biff – he's not lazy.

He goes on talking to himself as the lights come up on the boys' bedroom and we see them listening anxiously to the noise he is making and discussing his mental state. Happy describes how last week in the car he stopped at a green light and drove on when it turned red. At the end of their longish scene together we see Willy talking to an imaginary point off-stage. He is advising Biff about not making promises to girls, and advising Happy about how to clean the car. This is not just a device to give the boys time to change their costumes. It bridges very effectively into the first sequence from the past which is acted out and (in contrast to the present in which Willy's relationship with both sons is so bad) it shows the happiness of a frictionless family group, the sons proud of their father, the father proud of his sons. Instead of the single swift slide of deterioration we get in the relationship between Joe Keller and Chris, here Miller can give us any number of sharp juxtapositions of past and present, creating a pattern which will illuminate whatever facets of the changing relationship he wishes it to.

At the same time, this method gives an ironic context to the main action in the present tense which shows how dominated by the past both Willy and the boys are. When Willy goes to see his young boss, Howard Wagner, all he can do is talk of the past and the promises that old man Wagner, who is now dead, once made to him. Biff goes to see Bill Oliver because he remembers or thinks he remembers promises made to him when he worked for him before. Both father and son are still making the same kind of mistake they have always made. Though *Death of a Salesman* is by no means an Ibsenian play about imprisonment within the past, Willy cannot escape from his own pattern and Biff cannot escape from the pattern Willy has imposed on him.

Biff has quite forgotten that he left Bill Oliver under the shadow of having stolen a carton of basketballs. We do not get this incident

Arthur Miller

enacted but the mixture of incidents we do get gives us a clear view of how Biff's kleptomania has developed from its comparatively innocent beginnings and how it is largely Willy's fault. He has loved his sons too indulgently to impose any discipline on them. In this first scene from the past we see Biff carrying a new ball.

BIFF: The coach told me to practise my passing.

WILLY: That so? And he gave you the ball, heh?

BIFF: Well, I borrowed it from the locker room. [*He laughs confidentially.*]

WILLY [*laughing with him at the theft*]: I want you to return that.

HAPPY: I told you he wouldn't like it!

BIFF [*angrily*]: Well, I'm bringing it back!

WILLY [*stopping the incipient argument, to* HAPPY]: Sure he's gotta practise with a regulation ball, doesn't he? [*To* BIFF] Coach'll probably congratulate you on your initiative!

BIFF: Oh, he keeps congratulating my initiative all the time, Pop.

WILLY: That's because he likes you. If somebody else took that ball there'd be an uproar.

Later, in another scene from the past, we see Willy making Biff and Happy show off in front of their uncle Ben and he encourages Biff to steal wood from a building site. And now, when Biff goes to see Bill Oliver again after a gap of ten years, he ruins his chances with him – if he ever had any – by stealing a fountain pen from his desk.

In the same scene in the restaurant where the two boys have arranged to take Willy out to a celebration dinner, there is a passage in Happy's conversation with the waiter, Stanley, which, as several critics have pointed out, indicates a sympathy with the Marxist view that commerce, like property, is a form of theft.

HAPPY: It's a little celebration. My brother is – I think he pulled off a big deal today. I think we're going into business together.

STANLEY: Great! That's the best for you. Because a family business, you know what I mean? – that's the best.

HAPPY: That's what I think.

STANLEY: 'Cause what's the difference? Somebody steals? It's in the family. Know what I mean?

How much Miller sympathizes with this view is left open. We are not entitled to assume – as some critics do – that his own feelings coincide with the waiter's. Certainly some connection will be formed in the audience's mind between this allusion to stealing and the stealing that Biff does when he tries to make himself a career in business, but the montage method always leaves the audience free – sometimes too free – to draw its own inferences from the associations and juxtapositions. Here there is a slightly worrying ambiguity about whether some form of thieving would be inevitable for Biff in any business career.

The life that he and Happy would like is a life in the open air, playing games or using their well-developed bodies in manual work. Biff's visit to Bill Oliver is prompted partly by a fantasy in which he and Happy visualize themselves as running two teams to play games against each other to promote Oliver's sporting goods.

HAPPY: You and I, Biff – we have a line, the Loman Line. We train a couple of weeks, and put on a couple of exhibitions, see?

WILLY: That's an idea!

HAPPY: Wait! We form two basketball teams, see? Two water-polo teams. We play each other. It's a million dollars' worth of publicity. Two brothers, see? The Loman Brothers. Displays in the Royal Palms – all the hotels. And banners over the ring and the basketball court: 'Loman Brothers'. Baby, we could sell sporting goods!

WILLY: That is a one-million-dollar idea!

LINDA: Marvellous!

BIFF: I'm in great shape as far as that's concerned.

HAPPY: And the beauty of it is, Biff, it wouldn't be like a business. We'd be out playin' ball again . . .

BIFF [enthused]: Yeah, that's . . .

WILLY: Million-dollar . . .

HAPPY: And you wouldn't get fed up with it, Biff. It'd be the family again. There'd be the old honour, and comradeship, and if you wanted to go off for a swim or somethin' – well you'd do it! Without some smart cooky gettin' up ahead of you!

WILLY: Lick the world! You guys together could absolutely lick the civilized world.

BIFF: I'll see Oliver tomorrow. Hap, if we could work that out . . .

LINDA: Maybe things are beginning to –

It is apt that Willy and Linda are both in on the hatching of this hare-brained scheme, which Oliver could not realistically be expected to finance. But the characters are incapable of realism. They are all like salesmen who have swallowed their own line of sales talk. Biff has come to believe what he has told everybody else – that Oliver liked him and has invited him to come back if ever he needs help. It is only when he actually goes back, to find that Oliver hardly remembers him, that he realizes he never worked for him as a salesman, only as a shipping clerk.

To put this in perspective, Miller uses Charley and his son Bernard. Measured against Charley, Willy looks more impressive and more likable, but he comes to depend on Charley who 'lends' him fifty dollars a week to take home as salary. In the schoolboy scenes, the Loman brothers are more impressive and more likable than the studious Bernard, though even then they need his help in their school work and later, when Willy goes to Charley's office to borrow money, he meets the mature Bernard, married and successful and just on his way to Washington to plead a case in front of the Supreme Court. Like his father and unlike the Lomans, he is not a talker.

WILLY [as CHARLEY takes out his wallet]: The Supreme Court! And he didn't even mention it!

CHARLEY [counting out money on the desk]: He don't have to – he's gonna do it.

WILLY: And you never told him what to do, did you? You never took any interest in him.

The other yardstick against which Willy is measured is his elder brother Ben. Never having seen much of his father, Willy tries to erect Ben into a father figure, but he is incapable of taking his advice or following his example. Ben is not a victim of the industrial society. In him the pioneer spirit still survives and his appearance in Act Two reminds Willy of his lost opportunity when Ben offered him an open-air job in Alaska. Miller is not content to present Willy as a passive victim of society: he is given a choice and opts to stay where he is.

BEN: Now, look here, William. I've bought timberland in Alaska and I need a man to look after things for me.

WILLY: God, timberland! Me and my boys in those grand outdoors!

BEN: You've a new continent at your doorstep, William. Get out of these cities, they're full of talk and time payments and courts of law. Screw on your fists and you can fight for a fortune up there.

WILLY: Yes, yes! Linda, Linda!

[LINDA *enters as of old, with the wash.*]

LINDA: Oh, you're back?

BEN: I haven't much time.

WILLY: No, wait! Linda, he's got a proposition for me in Alaska.

LINDA: But you've got – [*To* BEN] He's got a beautiful job here.

WILLY: But in Alaska, kid, I could –

LINDA: You're doing well enough, Willy!

BEN [*to* LINDA]: Enough for what, my dear?

LINDA [*frightened of* BEN *and angry at him*]: Don't say those things to him! Enough to be happy right here, right now. [*To* WILLY, *while* BEN *laughs*] Why must everybody conquer the world? You're well liked, and the boys love you, and some-day – [*to* BEN] – why, old man Wagner told him just the other day that if he keeps it up he'll be a member of the firm, didn't he, Willy?

WILLY: Sure, sure. I am building something with this firm, Ben, and if a man is building something he must be on the right track, mustn't he?

The hard cadences of Ben's speech emphasize his toughness and his determination; the anxious rhythms of Willy's speech in this scene accurately capture the uncertainty of a man who is trying to sell ideas that have already been sold to him.

As Henry Popkin has pointed out, the references to nature and manual work 'form the chief repository of Miller's positive values'. According to Popkin, though, 'these bits of talk and action ... are brief and not entirely coherent.' To me it seems that they are quite sufficiently coherent and no more fragmentary (or brief) than the form of the play requires them to be. With its nightmarish shuttlings between present and past, the play may seem less coherent than *All*

Arthur Miller

My Sons. In fact it is less tightly but more powerfully structured and the montage is thoroughly germane to Miller's purposes. It is because of the structure and the development of situation which it encourages that the language is seldom disappointing as it so often was at the climaxes of *All My Sons*.

One scene which demands powerful language is the late-night seed-planting scene at the end of the play. Finally aware that he has ignored for too long the call of the open air, Willy pathetically tries to plant seeds by torchlight. Had the dialogue been weakly written, this scene would merely have made him look ludicrous. Instead, madly talking to his dead brother, he is almost like a salesman-Lear on a garden-heath. The poetry spreads from the action to the language, which is simple, unpretentious, innocent of any rhetorical inflation, but pregnant, specific, and thoroughly effective.

> *He is carrying a flashlight, a hoe, and a handful of seed pack-ets. He raps the top of the hoe sharply to fix it firmly, and then moves to the left, measuring off the distance with his foot. He holds the flashlight to look at the seed packets, reading off the instructions. He is in the blue of night.*

WILLY: Carrots ... quarter-inch apart. Rows ... one foot rows. [*He measures it off.*] One foot. [*He puts down a package and measures off.*] Beets. [*He puts down another package and measures again.*] Lettuce. [*He reads the package, puts it down.*] One foot – [*He breaks off as* BEN *appears at the right and moves slowly down to him.*] What a proposition, ts, ts. Terrific, terrific. 'Cause she's suffered, Ben, the woman has suffered. You understand me? A man can't go out the way he came in, Ben, a man has got to add up to something. You can't, you can't – [BEN *moves toward him as though to interrupt.*] You gotta consider, now. Don't answer so quick. Remember, it's a guaranteed twenty-thousand-dollar proposition. Now look, Ben, I want you to go through the ins and outs of this thing with me. I've got nobody to talk to, Ben, and the woman has suffered, you hear me?

Unfortunately, not all the writing is on this level. Linda, the patient, loyal wife and Charley, the patient, loyal neighbour, neither of whom are developed to their full potential as characters, both have

36

In the foreground on the left of picture, Joseph Calleia as JOE KELLER, Margalo Gillmore as KATE and Richard Leech as CHRIS in *All My Sons* at the Lyric, Hammersmith.

Katharine Alexander as LINDA, Paul Muni as WILLIE LOMAN and Kevin

flatly rhetorical speeches in defence of Willy. Linda's comes in Act One:

> I don't say he's a great man. Willy Loman never made a lot of money. His name was never in the paper. He's not the finest character that ever lived. But he's a human being and a terrible thing is happening to him. So attention must be paid. He's not to be allowed to fall into his grave like an old dog. Attention, attention must be finally paid to such a person. You called him crazy –

Charley's comes in the requiem at the end of the play:

> Nobody dast blame this man. You don't understand; Willy was a salesman. And for a salesman, there is no rock bottom to the life. He don't put a bolt to a nut, he don't tell you the law or give you medicine. He's a man way out there in the blue, riding on a smile and a shoeshine. And when they start not smiling back – that's an earthquake. And then you get yourself a couple of spots on your hat, and you're finished. Nobody dast blame this man. A salesman is got to dream, boy. It comes with the territory.

Both speeches provide glosses on Willy which are quite unnecessary. He himself provides everything we need to know about him in order to judge him, and because they are both redundant, neither speech is sufficiently related to (or supported by) action.

When Willy himself uses rhetorical language, as he sometimes does, there is a built-in irony which puts it in focus. In his speech about Biff at the end of Act One, for instance, the inadequacy of the words to fill out the idea points to the wrongness of the idea:

> Like a young god. Hercules – something like that. And the sun, the sun all around him. Remember how he waved to me? Right up from the field, with the representatives of three colleges standing by? And the buyers I brought, and the cheers when he came out – Loman, Loman, Loman! God Almighty, he'll be great yet. A star like that, magnificent, can never really fade away!

There is also an effective irony in juxtaposing this speech with Biff's discovery of the rubber tubing behind the gas stove in the kitchen and his realization that Willy is planning to kill himself. But there is no irony in Linda's and Charley's speeches. They are both selling the salesman to the audience.

Another facet of the crystal which is frequently illuminated by the montage of scenes is the relationship between sexual activity and guilt. Eric Bentley has suggested that the use of sex serves to mask the social criticism in the play and to offer an alternative explanation of the disasters that befall the protagonists. I would say, on the contrary, that all through the play Miller uses sex as a means of carrying his social argument forward. Willy, Biff and Happy all behave badly over sexual relationships and in each case Miller demonstrates very effectively how the bad behaviour both reflects their social conditioning and expresses their resentment of the role society forces them to play.

The failure of Willy's relationship with Linda is closely linked to his failure as a salesman. He believes, wrongly, that he needs to sell himself to her, to impress her by big talk. Even at the time he was doing relatively well, he was barely able to keep ahead of their hire-purchase commitments, but he always talked as though he were doing better than he really was. In spite of her love, she was never able to convince him that he was good enough for her as he actually was, in himself, and it was partly his failure to impress her as much as he felt she needed to be impressed that drove him into the arms of other women. To them he could boast without having his bluff called. So he sold himself to them with wisecracks and gifts of silk stockings.

Happy, who like Biff has been blown 'full of hot air' by Willy all through his childhood, knows that he can outbox, outrun and outlift anyone in the store. He resents having to work under men who are physically his inferiors and he revenges himself by seducing their fiancées.

> Sure, the guy's in line for the vice-presidency of the store. I don't know what gets into me, maybe I just have an over-developed sense of competition or something, but I went and ruined her, and furthermore I can't get rid of her. And he's the third executive I've done that to. Isn't that a crummy characteristic? And to top it all, I go to their weddings!

The two major sequences involving sex are Willy's affair with The Woman and the boys' episode with the two girls in the restaurant. Willy's affair is in the past but it gets brought powerfully into the present, particularly during the restaurant scene.

The importance of the infidelity to Linda is judged mainly in terms of the effect it has on Biff. This is shown very skilfully. Bernard, when he meets Willy in his father's office, is curious to know what it was that stopped Biff from trying to qualify for university. At school he only failed in one subject and he could have made this up by going to summer school. Bernard knows that something happened in Boston, where Biff went to visit Willy, which was a turning point in his life, for afterwards he adamantly refused to enroll for summer school. We do not find out what it was that happened until after we have seen Biff and Happy in action with the two girls. Happy's way of chatting them up is a simple application of the principles of salesmanship. He gets into conversation with the first girl by pretending to be a champagne salesman and telling the co-operative waiter to bring her a bottle of what he says is his brand. On Biff's arrival, Happy persuades her to ask a girl-friend to come along by selling Biff to her as a great football player. His conversation is full of sales-talky wisecracks.

When Willy arrives at the restaurant, he has just been sacked and, as in the earlier scene with Charley, he is living partly in the past. Interspersed through his conversation with the boys are lines which flash him (and us) back to the hotel in Boston. The Woman is first heard laughing off-stage and then heard speaking lines from off-stage, but we do not see her until after Willy has hit Biff and after Biff and Happy have gone off with the two girls.

In actuality Willy is now in the washroom of the restaurant; in his mind he is in the Boston hotel bedroom with The Woman. The knocking on the door is both nightmarish and expressive of guilt, like the knocking after the murder in *Macbeth*. Willy first denies that there is any knocking and when he finally has to open the door, it is Biff. By now, Willy has hidden The Woman in the bathroom and he has every chance of getting rid of Biff before she comes out, but characteristically, after telling him to go and wait downstairs, in his giggling admiration of the boy, he encourages him to repeat an imitation he has done of a schoolmaster. When The Woman starts laughing

Arthur Miller

in the bathroom and comes out half-naked, nothing Willy says or does can help. The experience is traumatic for Biff – just as if he were much younger than he actually is. The jerk back into the present tense leaves Willy on his knees in the washroom.

It is ironical and touching that immediately after this re-enactment of Willy's infidelity, we see Linda's loyalty to him in the implacable scorn she shows towards her two sons after their behaviour to Willy in the restaurant. The language is straightforward, but unlike the more ambitious language of *All My Sons*, it reaches the necessary level of intensity:

> BIFF: I stole myself out of every good job since high school!
> WILLY: And whose fault is that?
> BIFF: And I never got anywhere because you blew me so full of hot air I could never stand taking orders from anybody! That's whose fault it is!
> WILLY: I hear that!
> LINDA: Don't, Biff!
> BIFF: It's goddam time you heard that! I had to be boss big shot in two weeks, and I'm through with it!
> WILLY: Then hang yourself! For spite, hang yourself!
> BIFF: No! Nobody's hanging himself, Willy! I ran down eleven flights with a pen in my hand today. And suddenly I stopped, you hear me? And in the middle of that office building, do you hear this? I stopped in the middle of that building and I saw – the sky. I saw the things that I love in this world. The work and the food and time to sit and smoke. And I looked at the pen and said to myself, what the hell am I grabbing this for? Why am I trying to become what I don't want to be? What am I doing in an office, making a contemptuous, begging fool of myself, when all I want is out there, waiting for me the minute I say I know who I am! Why can't I say that, Willy? [*He tries to make* WILLY *face him, but* WILLY *pulls away and moves to the left.*]
> WILLY [*with hatred, threateningly*]: The door of your life is wide open!
> BIFF: Pop! I'm a dime a dozen, and so are you!
> WILLY [*turning on him now in an uncontrolled outburst*]: I am not a dime a dozen! I am Willy Loman, and you are Biff Loman!

[BIFF *starts for* WILLY, *but is blocked by* HAPPY. *In his fury,* BIFF *seems on the verge of attacking his father.*]

BIFF: I am not a leader of men, Willy, and neither are you. You were never anything but a hard-working drummer who landed in the ash-can like all the rest of them! I'm one dollar an hour, Willy! I tried seven states and couldn't raise it. A buck an hour! Do you gather my meaning? I'm not bringing home any prizes any more, and you're going to stop waiting for me to bring them home!

WILLY [*directly to* BIFF]: You vengeful, spiteful mut!

[BIFF *breaks from* HAPPY, WILLY, *in fright, starts up the stairs.* BIFF *grabs him.*]

BIFF [*at the peak of his fury*]: Pop, I'm nothing! I'm nothing, Pop. Can't you understand that? There's no spite in it any more. I'm just what I am, that's all.

[BIFF'S *fury has spent itself, and he breaks down, sobbing, holding on to* WILLY, *who dumbly fumbles for* BIFF'S *face.*]

WILLY [*astonished*]: What're you doing? What're you doing? [*To* LINDA.] Why is he crying?

BIFF [*crying, broken*]: Will you let me go, for Christ's sake? Will you take that phony dream and burn it before something happens? [*Struggling to contain himself, he pulls away and moves to the stairs.*] I'll go in the morning. Put him – put him to bed. [*Exhausted,* BIFF *moves up the stairs to his room.*]

WILLY [*after a long pause, astonished, elevated*]: Isn't that – isn't that remarkable? Biff – he likes me!

It is worth quoting Arthur Miller's explanation of how Willy is driven to his death by this revelation of love:

In this he is given his existence, so to speak – his fatherhood, for which he has always striven and which until now he could not achieve. That he is unable to take victory thoroughly to his heart, that it closes the circle for him and propels him to his death, is the wage of his sin, which was to have committed himself so completely to the counterfeits of dignity and the false coinage embodied in his idea of success that he can prove his existence only by bestowing 'power' on his posterity, a power deriving from the sale of his last asset, himself, for the price of his insurance policy.

I must confess here to a miscalculation, however . . . I did not realize either how few would be impressed by the fact that this man is actually a very brave spirit who cannot settle for half but must pursue his dream of himself to the end . . . Had Willy been unaware of his separation from values that endure he would have died contentedly while polishing his car, probably on a Sunday afternoon with the ball game coming over the radio. But he was agonized by his awareness of being in a false position, so constantly haunted by the hollowness of all he had placed his faith in, so aware, in short, that he must somehow be filled in his spirit or fly apart, that he staked his very life on the ultimate assertion.

This analysis of what it is that makes Willy into an effective tragic hero also has its bearing on John Proctor in *The Crucible* and Eddie Carbone in *A View from the Bridge*, who are also brave and also unable to 'settle for half'.

But Willy is different in that his death is both something with a cash value and an idea that he has to sell himself. Altogether the selling in the play proves to be a much more useful dramatic currency than the 'pipe-dreams' in Eugene O'Neill's *The Iceman Cometh*, to which it is roughly comparable. But in the selling, the words are always far more closely welded to action.

THE CRUCIBLE

Structurally *The Crucible* is as different from *Death of a Salesman* as *Death of a Salesman* is from *All My Sons*. Miller returns to a chronological narrative but taking a bigger cast of characters and moving between different locales. The hero, instead of being representative of his society, stands out against it, and dies because (unlike Willy Loman) he is not sufficiently separated from values that endure. Like Shaw's St. Joan he is so eager to stay alive that he makes the 'confession' that is required of him, only to tear it up afterwards, knowing that if he puts his name to it he will never 'find himself' again. Identity is more precious than survival.

Ranged against him is almost the whole of Salem society, which Miller rightly shows both before and during the witch hunt. In the first few minutes of action he establishes a strong and suspenseful situation. Rev. Parris's young daughter Betty is lying in a stupor and Rev. Hale, a specialist in diabolical possession, is on his way over. After this, the play can afford a passage of more leisurely dialogue to build up a quick picture of a Puritan community in which the acquisitive urge is as strong as the religious and in which the soil is ready for a witch hunt which thrusts down such powerful roots so frighteningly quickly.

As Arthur Miller has said:

> The central impulse for writing . . . was not the social but the interior psychological question, which was the question of that guilt residing in Salem which the hysteria merely unleashed, but did not create.

The play was written before he was himself a victim of McCarthyism, but he was already aware that what was driving the conformists to join in the witch hunt was a sense of their own guilt and a panicky desire to cover it up. The pattern in Salem was the same, as Miller indicates by the way he uses his large cast of supporting characters. Rev. Parris suffers from a persecution complex. Giles Cory is suspicious of his wife because she reads books. Ann Putnam, who has lost

Arthur Miller

seven babies within a day of giving birth to them, is eager to think that unnatural causes are at work, and the predatory Thomas Putnam is always litigating against his neighbours. Superstition and acrimony are rife and the sermons are mostly about hellfire.

The spacing out of the four sequences which make up the play's four acts is determined largely by the necessity of showing how the forces of terrorization join together. After its quiet beginning, the first act ends hysterically with Tituba, the Negress slave, Abigail, the ring-leader of the trouble-makers, and Betty all denouncing other women in order to protect themselves. And before it reaches this climax, it shows us in Rev. Hale's cross-examination of Abigail and Tituba, how the outlines of truth can dissolve in the smokescreen of instant fiction that both of them throw out in self-defence.

HALE: You cannot evade me, Abigail – Did your cousin drink any of the brew in that kettle?

ABIGAIL: She never drank it!

HALE: Did you drink it?

ABIGAIL: No, sir!

HALE: Did Tituba ask you to drink it?

ABIGAIL: She tried but I refused.

HALE: *Why* are you concealing? Have you sold yourself to Lucifer?

ABIGAIL: I never sold myself! I'm a good girl – I – [*Ann enters with Tituba*]. I did drink of the kettle! – She made me do it! She made Betty do it!

TITUBA: Abby!

ABIGAIL: She makes me drink blood!

PARRIS: Blood!!

ANN: My baby's blood?

TITUBA: No – no, chicken blood, I give she chicken blood!

HALE: Woman, have you enlisted these children for the Devil?

TITUBA: No – no, sir, I don't truck with the Devil!

HALE [*of Betty*]: Why can she not wake? Are you silencing this child?

TITUBA: I love me Betty!

HALE: You have sent your spirit out upon this child, have you not? Are you gathering souls for the Devil?

ABIGAIL: She send her spirit on me in *church*, she make me laugh at *prayer*!

44

PARRIS: She have often laughed at prayer!

ABIGAIL: She comes to me every night to go and drink blood!

TITUBA: You beg *me* to conjure, Abby! She beg *me* make charm —

ABIGAIL: I'll tell you something. She comes to me while I sleep; she's always making me dream corruptions!

TITUBA: Abby!

ABIGAIL [*at* RIGHT *of Betty's head. Hysterically, horrified*]: Sometimes I wake and find myself standing in the open doorway and not a stitch on my body! (*Covering herself with her arms, turning up stage and away.*] I always hear her laughing in my sleep. I hear her singing her Barbados songs and tempting me with —

TITUBA: Mister Reverend, I never — } [*Together.*]
HALE: Tituba, I want you to wake this child.

TITUBA: I have no power on this child, sir.

HALE: You most certainly do, and you will loose her from it now! When did you compact with the Devil?

TITUBA: I don't compact with no Devil!

PARRIS: You will confess yourself or I will take you out and whip you to your death, Tituba!

PUTNAM: This woman must be hanged! She must be taken and hanged!

TITUBA [*kneeling*]: No – no, don't hang Tituba. I tell him I don't desire to work for him, sir.

Act Two not only shows how the court has come into existence: we see how Mary Warren has come to convince herself that she has grounds for denouncing Sarah Good.

MARY: She tried to kill me many times, Goody Proctor!

ELIZABETH: Why, I never heard you mention that before.

MARY [*innocently*]: I never *knew* it before. I never knew anything before. When she come into the court I say to myself, I must not accuse this woman, for she sleep in ditches, and so very old and poor. . . . But then . . . then she sit there, denying and denying, and I feel a misty coldness climbin' up my back, and the skin on my skull begin to creep, and I feel a clamp around my neck and I cannot breathe air; and then . . . [*Entranced as though it were a miracle.*] I hear a voice, a screamin' voice, and it were *my* voice . . . and all at once I

Arthur Miller

> remembered everything she done to me! [*Slight pause as Proctor watches Elizabeth pass him, then speaks, being aware of Elizabeth's alarm.*]
>
> PROCTOR [*looking at Elizabeth*]: Why? – What did she do to you?
>
> MARY [*like one awakened to a marvellous secret insight*]: So many time, Mister Proctor, she come to this very door beggin' bread and a cup of cider – and mark *this* – whenever I turned her away empty – she *mumbled*.

Despite finding the girl unsympathetic, Miller projects himself imaginatively into her mental processes.

In Act Three he uses her again to give a subtle analysis of how she and the others put on a performance of diabolical possession. When she admits that she had only been pretending to faint in the court, Danforth, the judge, counters by asking her to faint now. Like an actress unable to go into an emotional scene without warming up, she cannot. But when, at the end of the act, Abigail fights Proctor's denunciation of her as a whore by staging a new bout of demoniac possession, Mary not only joins in but outscreams the others.

This act also initiates us into the workings and into the psychology of the court itself. Like so many other organizations, it is concerned above all with its own survival and acts most savagely when in danger of being discredited. Miller makes an important point very theatrically when he shows how the prompt arrangements for the arrest of all ninety-one signatories of the petition effectively inhibit anyone of any conscience from producing witnesses in case they too are arrested.

It is a remarkable achievement on Miller's part to write dialogue which is so acceptable as belonging to the seventeenth century and which is so flexible. Sometimes the language is simple and functional; sometimes it is picturesque with images jostling densely against each other. This is Abigail bullying the other girls into submission:

> Now look you. All of you. We danced. And Tituba conjured Ruth Putnam's dead sisters. And that is all. And mark this – let either of you breathe a word, or the edge of a word about the other things, and I will come to you in the black of some terrible night and I will bring a pointy reckoning that will shudder you. And you know I can do it; I saw Indians smash my dear parents'

heads on the pillow next to mine, and I have seen some reddish work done at night, and I can make you wish you had never seen the sun go down!

Sexual attraction between Abigail and Proctor is made far more vivid than it is between Chris and Ann in *All My Sons*, partly because of the tension created by Proctor's refusal to give in to his instincts, but mainly because of the language.

> ABIGAIL: I have a sense for heat, John, and yours has drawn me to my window. Do you tell me you've never looked up at my window?
> PROCTOR: Perhaps I . . . have.
> ABIGAIL: I know you, John, I *know* you. [*She is weeping.*] I cannot sleep for dreamin', I cannot dream but I wake and walk about the house as though I'd find you comin' through some door.
> PROCTOR [*taking her hands*]: Child . . .
> ABIGAIL [*with a flash of anger. Throwing his hands off*]: How do you call me child!

When he becomes rhetorical, as he does when Elizabeth is arrested, the period flavour helps the rhetoric.

> PROCTOR: If *she* is innocent! Why do you never wonder if Parris be innocent, or Abigail? Is the accuser always holy now? Were they born this morning as clean as God's fingers? I'll tell you what's walking Salem – vengeance is walking Salem. We are what we always were in Salem, but now the little crazy children are jangling the keys of the kingdom, and common vengeance writes the law! This warrant's vengeance; I will not give my wife to vengeance!

In the original version of the play, the level of the writing was consistently maintained, but six months after the New York opening, Miller rewrote some of Proctor's part, introducing several rather jarring purple passages. The scene with Elizabeth at the beginning of Act Two suffers and there is a seriously damaging lapse at the end of the play, just after he has torn up his confession. Here is the original version:

> HALE: Man, you will hang! – You cannot!

Arthur Miller

PROCTOR [*crossing slowly* RIGHT *to Elizabeth, takes her hands for a moment. Simply with dignity*]: Pray God it speaks some goodness for me. [*They embrace. He then holds her at arm's length.*] Give them no tear. Show them a heart of stone and sink them with it.

And here is the rewrite:

HALE: Man, you will hang! You cannot!
PROCTOR [*his eyes full of tears*]: I can. And there's your first marvel, that I can. You have made your magic now, for now I do think I see some shred of goodness in John Proctor. Not enough to weave a banner with, but white enough to keep it from such dogs. [ELIZABETH, *in a burst of terror, rushes to him and weeps against his hand.*] Give them no tear! Tears pleasure them! Show honour now, show a stony heart and sink them with it! [*He has lifted her, and kisses her now with great passion.*]

Another change he made at this time was to cut out the scene in which Proctor and Abigail meet at night in a wood. This came between Elizabeth's arrest and the scene in the anteroom of the court, and it showed Abigail as crazed to the point of believing in her own fiction.

ABIGAIL: I cannot bear lewd looks no more, John. My spirit's changed entirely. I ought be given Godly looks when I suffer for them as I do.
PROCTOR: Oh? How do you suffer, Abby?
ABIGAIL [*pulls up dress*]: Why, look at my leg. I'm holes all over from their damned needles and pins. [*Touching her stomach.*] The jab your wife gave me's not healed yet, y'know.
PROCTOR [*seeing her madness now*]: Oh, it isn't.
ABIGAIL: I think sometimes she pricks it open again while I sleep.

This is not altogether satisfactory and it makes us see her behaviour in the court in a very different light – as more spontaneous, less calculating. But without this scene, she remains underdeveloped and her disappearance at the end of the play leaves us unsatisfied.

Altogether the end is slightly disappointing, particularly in the new version. Apart from Proctor's rhetoric and Abigail's absence, the focus seems to have narrowed. There are some good touches at the beginning of the act (like the mention of cows wandering through the highroads) to give us an impression of how the whole community has been affected by the wholesale arrests. But afterwards the general light on the social background dims down until there seems to be nothing but an individual spot-light on Proctor.

A MEMORY OF TWO MONDAYS

Originally performed in a double bill with *A View from the Bridge* on Broadway in 1955, *A Memory of Two Mondays* remains the least known of Miller's mature plays, though he has himself said there is nothing in his Collected Plays that he loves better.

He prefaced the American edition of the two one-act pieces with an essay 'On Social Plays' in which he questions whether it would still be possible to create a true tragic figure.

> When men live, as they do under any industrialized system, as integers who have no weight, no *person*, excepting as either customers, draftees, machine tenders, ideologists, or whatever, it is unlikely (and in my opinion impossible) that a dramatic picture of them can really overcome the public knowledge of their nature in real life. In such a society, be it communistic or capitalistic, man is not tragic, he is pathetic. The tragic figure must have certain innate powers which he uses to pass over the boundaries of the known social law – the accepted mores of his people – in order to test and discover necessity. Such a quest implies that the individual who has moved on to that course must be somehow recognized by the law, by the mores, by the powers that design – as having the worth, the innate value, of a whole people asking a basic question and demanding its answer. We are so atomized socially that no character in a play can conceivably stand as our vanguard, as our heroic questioner.

In *A Memory of Two Mondays* he is not so much concerned to make an individual (like Willy Loman) stand for the society as to portray a small group of men who are representative of it. And whereas we never see Willy actually trying to sell anyone anything, here we see the men at work around the packing table of a large auto-parts warehouse. But it is not a realistic play. As Miller says:*

> For a moment I was striving not to make people forget they were in a theatre, not to obliterate an awareness of form, not to forge a pretence of life, but to be abrupt, clear, and explicit in setting forth fact as fact and art as art so that the sea of

* In his Introduction to the Collected Plays.

A Memory of Two Mondays

theatrical sentiment, which is so easily let in to drown all shape, meaning, and perspective, might be held back and some hard outline of a human dilemma be allowed to rise and stand. *A Memory of Two Mondays* has a story but not a plot, because the life it reflects appears to me to strip people of alternatives and will beyond a close and tight periphery in which they may exercise a meagre choice.

For the first time, he interpolates passages of verse into his dialogue. There are two verse sequences. The first comes during a stylized window-cleaning scene in which a change of light helps to denote the passage of time between the first Monday morning, which is in summer, to the second, which is in winter. The second verse sequence helps to preserve continuous action between the Monday and the Tuesday.

The pivotal character, Bert, a boy of eighteen, is modelled more directly on Miller himself than any of his other heroes (except Quentin in *After the Fall*). After doing very indifferently at school, Miller worked for two years in an automobile-parts warehouse to earn enough money to pay for his course at Michigan University. Bert got bad marks in high school.

> I just played ball and fooled around, that's all.
> I think I wasn't listening, y'know?

And he saves eleven or twelve dollars a week out of his fifteen dollar salary, hoping to get into college. Meanwhile he reads Tolstoy and the *New York Times*.

As in *The Crucible*, Miller shows great skill in handling a large cast, bringing each character separately to life at his first appearance. Raymond, the manager, is fairly unconcerned about anything except making the men get on with the job. Agatha is encouraging towards Bert. Patricia is attractive. Gus is likeably concerned that old Jim should not have to lift any of the heavy parts. Kenneth, an immigrant from Ireland, recites poetry with ironical humour and speaks longingly about the green countryside. Larry is so in love with the valves on his new car that he does not care how much he will lose on it when the time comes to sell. Frank, the lorry driver, has a good memory for baseball and a good list of telephone numbers so that he can fix a date in any district he has to deliver to.

Neat and colourful though all this characterization is, it is inevitably superficial. The only character to roar memorably into life is Gus, a bald, barrel-bellied Slav of sixty-eight who has worked in the warehouse for twenty-two years. He has not been home to his sick wife all week-end and he threatens to leave if they sack Tom Kelly, an alcoholic who has come to work in a stupor and not for the first time. But he has worked there for sixteen years. Miller leads up very well indeed to the climax of the first Monday. Tom has been summoned by Mr Eagle and Gus delivers his ultimatum just before hearing from a neighbour over the telephone that his wife has died.

Altogether, the liveliness of Gus as a character has exactly the right relationship to the deathliness of the job he has to do. We see how his loyalty to the others, his bursts of temper, his joking threats, his impulses and his values all derive from the life he lives. His whole personality is a comment on the system. With the others, Miller does not succeed quite so well in linking his characterization with his social commentary. Kenneth makes the point that after sixteen monotonous years in the warehouse, Tom cannot be blamed for drinking, and Larry complains that he has been asking for a five dollar rise for two years and needs the money. But Miller does not allow himself time or space to involve us sufficiently in their predicaments. Tom's alcoholic stupor is used chiefly as a cue for a lot of very funny stage business in which the others try to arrange his unresisting body to give Mr Eagle the impression that he is writing. Larry's financial predicament is elbowed out of the foreground by his relationship with Patricia, which progresses rapidly, thanks to the new car. But this too is treated almost too tersely to be dramatically worthwhile.

Had the poetry in the play been better, it could have helped to give everything else its proper perspective. But it is very inadequate.

> Gus, and Agnes, and Tommy and Larry, Jim and Patricia –
> Why does it make me so sad to see them every morning?
> It's like the subway;
> Every day I see the same people getting on
> And the same people getting off,

The courtroom scene in *The Crucible* at the Old Vic.

Alec Guinness as VON BERG, Anthony Quayle as LEDUC, David Calderisi as the GYPSY, Brian Blessed as BAYARD and Derek Smith as the PROFESSOR in *Incident at Vichy* at the Phoenix Theatre.

A Memory of Two Mondays

> And all that happens is that they get older. God!
> Sometimes it scares me; like all of us in the world
> Were riding back and forth across a great big room
> From wall to wall and back again,
> And no end ever! Just no end!

These lame lines, with their faint echoes of T. S. Eliot, fail completely
to make the point Miller makes in his Introduction to the Collected
Plays:

> I hoped to define for myself the value of hope, why it must
> arise, as well as the heroism of those who know, at least, how
> to endure its absence . . . from this endless environment, a
> boy emerges who will not accept its defeat or its mood as final,
> and literally takes himself off on a quest for a higher gratifica-
> tion.

The minor characters may be pathetic but Bert certainly cannot
stand as a heroic questioner. Only better verse and a fuller development of his character could have saved him from paling into insignifi-
cance beside the bawdy, raucous Gus. Possibly Gus should have been
given more of the centre of the stage and developed into more of a
'heroic questioner'. As it is, he is much less effective on the second
Monday than on the first and the news of his death on the Tuesday
does not pack the punch it ought to.

The prose is much better than the verse, and some of it, allowing
for the differences of the American idiom, and of the Slav and Irish
variants of it, almost gives a foretaste of Pinter. Certainly it attains
to a queer quality through its repetitiveness:

GUS: You crazy? Buy Auburn?
LARRY [*with depth – a profound conclusion*]: I like the valves,
    Gus.
GUS: Yeah, but when you gonna go sell it who gonna buy an
    Auburn?
LARRY: Didn't you ever get to where you don't care about that?
    I *always* liked those valves, and I decided, that's all.
GUS: Yeah, but when you gonna go sell it —
LARRY: I don't care.
GUS: You don't care!

Arthur Miller

> LARRY: I'm sick of dreaming about things. They've got the most beautifully laid-out valves in the country on that car, and I want it, that's all.
>
> [KENNETH *is weighing a package on the scales.*]
>
> GUS: Yeah, but when you gonna go sell it —
>
> LARRY: I just don't care, Gus.

And the best speech in the whole play is Gus's repetitious speech about how long he has been there.

> Them mice was here before you was born. [BERT *nods uncomfortably, full of sadness.*] When Mr Eagle was in high school I was already here. When there was Winton Six I was here. When was Minerva car I was here. When Stanley Steamer I was here, and Stearns Knight, and Marmon was good car; I was here all them times. I was here first day Raymond come; he was young boy; work hard be manager. When Agnes still think she was gonna get married I was here. When was Locomobile, and Model K Ford and Model N Ford – all them different Fords, and Franklin was good car, Jordan car, Reo car, Pierce Arrow, Cleveland car – all them was good cars. All them times I was here.

This contains the heart of the play and points to the heart of the problem of writing it. How long he has been there is the main point but most of the time he has been there, nothing dramatic or dramatizable has happened. The play, simply to keep the audience interested, has to belie its subject.

A VIEW FROM THE BRIDGE

In the original version of *A View from the Bridge* there is much more
verse than there is in *A Memory of Two Mondays* and most of it is
both very much better as verse and more integral to the drama.
Where Miller succeeds best of all is where he catches the character-
istic cadences of a speech and emphasizes the rhythm of it through the
verse. This is particularly effective where the character speaks an
idiosyncratic English, as Rodolpho does – a young Italian who has
only just arrived in America. There is great charm in his explanation
of why it is important to have a motorbike in Italy:

> Oh, no, the machine, the machine is necessary.
> A man comes into a great hotel and says,
> 'I am a messenger.' Who is this man?
> He disappears walking, there is no noise, nothing –
> Maybe he will never come back,
> Maybe he will never deliver the message.
> But a man who rides up on a great machine,
> This man is responsible, this man exists.
> He will be given messages.

What does not succeed is the verse of the lawyer Alfieri, which is
aimed at rooting the play deeper in the classical past:

> When the tide is right,
> And the wind blows the sea air against these houses,
> I sit here in my office,
> Thinking it is all so timeless here.
> I think of Sicily, from where these people came,
> The Roman rocks of Calabria,
> Siracusa on the cliffs, where Carthaginian and Greek
> Fought such bloody fights. I think of Hannibal,
> Who slew the fathers of these people; Caesar,
> Whipping them on in Latin.

The story does have a certain affinity with that of a Greek tragedy,
but Alfieri is not altogether successful as a chorus, especially in the
earlier part of the play, where he is not drawn into the action.

Arthur Miller

In the two-act version of the play, which Miller wrote for London, his verse – and all the other verse – is rewritten as prose. As in the two passages I have just quoted, most of the verse lines are end-stopped, so although the actor is likely to be less aware of the rhythm when the dialogue is printed as prose, the punctuation could be sufficient to lead him to the same result.

The two-act version of the play is not in fact very much longer than the one-act version. There are a few cuts in the Alfieri scenes and a few expansions of the other scenes but the interval probably adds as much to the running time as the extra dialogue does. But it helps the play hugely, by developing the dramatic potential of the story. As Miller put it himself:

> In writing this play originally I obeyed the impulse to indicate, to telegraph, so to speak, rather than to explore and exploit what at first had seemed to me the inevitable and therefore unnecessary emotional implications of the conflict

But he found out from watching performances in New York that the play had more to do with his personal preoccupations and personal experience than he had originally thought and his rewriting was accordingly less impersonal. He identified more, not only with Eddie, but also with Beatrice and Catherine.

The opening scene between Eddie and Catherine is expanded. In the earlier version, his possessiveness is only lightly touched in through the refusal to let her wear her new pair of shoes and in a four-speech conversation about getting a job. She says that the teacher has told her she could go to work now; Eddie says he wants her to wait until she is at least eighteen. In the later version she has actually been offered a job at fifty dollars a week in a plumbing company over Nostrand Avenue and the principal of the school is in favour of her taking it. Eddie objects to the area and shows that he prefers to go on supporting her but Beatrice, who is now made more overt in her concern about his relationship with her, talks him into changing his mind and there is a touching moment when Catherine responds with a burst of affection.

EDDIE [*with a sense of her childhood, her babyhood, and the years*]:
All right, go to work. [*She looks at him, then rushes and hugs*

him.] Hey, hey! Take it easy! [*He holds her face away from him to look at her.*] What're you cryin' about? [*He is affected by her, but smiles his emotion away.*]

CATHERINE [*sitting at her place*]: I just – [*Bursting out*] I'm gonna buy all new dishes with my first pay! [*They laugh warmly.*] I mean it. I'll fix up the whole house! I'll buy a rug!

EDDIE: And then you'll move away.

CATHERINE: No, Eddie!

EDDIE [*grinning*]: Why not? That's life. And you'll come visit on Sundays, then once a month, then Christmas and New Years, finally.

Miller is very good at building up a reservoir of warmth in his characters and tapping it like this, with a careful controlling hand on the flow of emotion from the tap.

The later version goes into slightly more detail about how the network brings the illegal immigrants into the country but the first scene with Marco and Rodolpho is barely altered, and neither is the scene with the two stevedores, nor the scene in which Rodolpho brings Catherine home from the cinema to find Eddie waiting jealously in the street. But this is now followed by a new conversation between Beatrice and Catherine, which strengthens Beatrice's character because it shows her making a much more determined fight than before to alter the status quo. She encourages Catherine to disregard Eddie's warning that if Rodolpho wants to marry her it is only to secure American citizenship, and in her efforts to bring Catherine to a more adult awareness and a more adult deportment of herself, we are now shown explicitly into the jealousy she feels herself at losing so much of Eddie's affection to the young girl.

BEATRICE: So you'll act different now, heh?

CATHERINE: Yeah, I will. I'll remember.

BEATRICE: Because it ain't only up to him, Katie, you understand? I told him the same thing already.

CATHERINE [*quickly*]: What?

BEATRICE: That he should let you go. But, you see, if only I tell him, he thinks I'm just bawlin' him out, or maybe I'm jealous or somethin', you know?

CATHERINE [*astonished*]: He said you was jealous?

BEATRICE: No, I'm just sayin' maybe that's what he thinks.

Arthur Miller

[*She reaches over to* CATHERINE's *hand; with a strained smile*]
You think I'm jealous of you, honey?

CATHERINE: No! It's the first I thought of it.

BEATRICE [*with a quiet sad laugh*]: Well you should have
thought of it before . . . but I'm not. We'll be all right. Just
give him to understand; you don't have to fight, you're just —
You're a woman, that's all, and you got a nice boy, and now
the time came when you said good-bye. All right?

CATHERINE [*strangely moved at the prospect*]: All right. . . . If I
can.

BEATRICE: Honey . . . you gotta.

And again, in the scene where Eddie protests to Marco about Rodolpho's behaviour with Catherine, Beatrice's involvement is deepened.

RODOLPHO: I have respect for her, Eddie. I do anything wrong?

EDDIE: Look, kid, I ain't her father, I'm only her uncle —

BEATRICE: Well then, be an uncle then. [EDDIE *looks at her,
aware of her criticizing force.*] I *mean.*

Another new line is written for her later, contributing to the excellent
build-up for what is now the curtain to Act One. Even at the climax,
though, the explosion is still kept well below the surface, exactly as
before. Eddie is in such a state of tension that he has to release some
of it and he cannot resist the opportunity he has created for himself,
under pretext of teaching Rodolpho how to box, of hitting him in the
face. Rodolpho, who has previously been cautious not to provoke
Eddie, retaliates by dancing with Catherine in front of him and the
climax of the next act, at which Marco is to kill Eddie, is anticipated
by the minatory moment when Marco, after challenging Eddie to lift
a chair by gripping the bottom of one of its legs, and finding that he
can't, lifts it himself and holds it over his head like a weapon. It is a
striking theatrical moment.

The scene between Catherine and Rodolpho which is to culminate
in love-making works very well, as before, with the pleasing cadences
of Rodolpho's speech trapped almost equally tellingly in prose and
with Catherine's loyalty to Eddie making her feel awkward about
loving Rodolpho. But in this version, she is more critical of Beatrice.

If I was a wife I would make a man happy instead of goin' at him all the time. I can tell a block away when he's blue in his mind and just wants to talk to somebody quiet and nice. . . . I can tell when he's hungry or wants beer before he even says anything. I know when his feet hurt him, I mean I *know* him and now I'm supposed to turn around and make a stranger out of him?

And when Eddie returns unexpectedly early, the conflict is filled out:

CATHERINE [*trembling with fright*]: I think I have to get out of here, Eddie.

EDDIE: No, you ain't goin' nowheres, he's the one.

CATHERINE: I think I can't stay here no more. I'm sorry, Eddie. [*She sees the tears in his eyes.*] Well, don't cry. I'll be around the neighbourhood; I'll see you. I just can't stay here no more. You know I can't. [*Her sobs of pity and love for him break her composure.*] Don't you know I can't? You know that, don't you? [*She goes to him.*] Wish me luck. [*She clasps her hands prayerfully.*] Oh, Eddie, don't be like that!

EDDIE: You ain't goin' nowheres.

CATHERINE: Eddie, I'm not gonna be a baby any more! You — [*He reaches out suddenly, draws her to him, and as she strives to free herself he kisses her on the mouth.*]

In the earlier version, this was only sketched in:

EDDIE: Pack it up. Go ahead. Get your stuff and get outa here. [CATHERINE *puts down the iron and walks towards the bedroom, and* EDDIE *grabs her arm.*] Where you goin'?

CATHERINE: Don't bother me, Eddie. I'm goin' with him.

EDDIE: You goin' with him. You goin' with him, heh? [*He grabs her face in the vice of his two hands.*] You goin' with him! [*He kisses her on the mouth as she pulls at his arms; he will not let go, keeps his face pressed against hers.*]

The climax, too, is better managed now. Beatrice is given an explicit line

You want somethin' else, Eddie, and you can never have her!

which helps to exploit the full dramatic potential of the situation, and Eddie's speech – one of his few speeches to be written originally as verse – is better as prose.

Arthur Miller

EDDIE [– *he gradually comes to address the people*]: Maybe he comes to apologize to me. Heh, Marco? For what you said about me in front of the neighbourhood? [*He is incensing himself and little bits of laughter even escape him as his eyes are murderous and he cracks his knuckles in his hands with a strange sort of relaxation.*] He knows that ain't right. To do like that? To a man? Which I put my roof over their head and my food in their mouth? Like in the Bible? Strangers I never seen in my whole life? To come out of the water and grab a girl for a passport? To go and take from your own family like from the stable -- and never a word to me? And now accusations in the bargain! [*Directly to* MARCO]. Wipin' the neighbourhood with my name like a dirty rag! I want my name, Marco. [*He is moving now, carefully towards* MARCO.] Now gimme my name and we go together to the wedding.

Like Proctor, he will die for his name and, like Joe Keller, he has been betrayed by the law of his own nature into breaking the law of his duty to humanity. He has violated the accepted mores of his people out of a necessity created by an illegitimate passion. As Alfieri says in the later version of his final speech,

Most of the time now we settle for half and I like it better. But the truth is holy, and even as I know how wrong he was, and his death useless, I tremble, for I confess that something perversely pure calls to me from his memory – not purely good, but himself purely, for he allowed himself to be wholly known and for that I think I will love him more than all my sensible clients.

AFTER THE FALL

Between the two-act version of *A View from the Bridge*, which was produced in London in October 1956 and *After the Fall*, which was the first play to be produced at the Lincoln Centre (in January 1964) there was a gap of over seven years during which Arthur Miller wrote nothing for the stage, though in 1961 he wrote the screenplay for *The Misfits*, based on a short story he had published in 1957.

After the Fall is a failure, but a much more interesting one than most critics have allowed. It was his most experimental play since *Death of a Salesman* and it is unfortunate that the hostile reaction to it may have deterred him from making further formal experiments. It returns to the idea he had tried out in his original draft of *Death of a Salesman* – setting the whole action inside the chief character's head.

At the Lincoln Centre, the open stage made it impossible for people to appear and disappear abruptly as they do in the mind but in the production which Franco Zeffirelli directed in Italy,* the acting area was contained in concentric oblong steel frames which receded towards the centre and which were covered at the sides like the inside of a camera. Actors could make entrances or exits at any of the openings in the covering and, thanks to the pneumatic lifts, they could appear at any height. When needed, the suggestion of a concentration camp was produced by a certain play of light on the girders of the steel frame. In New York, the stone tower dominated the stage as Miller's stage direction prescribes.

The failure of the play is its failure to justify the use of this image. The story is about a man who fought as hard as he could against having to become what he called a Separate Person. The central relationship poses the question of whether a symbiotic relationship is possible between two people like Quentin and Maggie. A woman whose innocence has not been destroyed by the innumerable men who have taken advantage of it, she seems capable of absolute trust, total devotion.

* Miller has described it in his interview in *The Paris Review*, Summer 1966.

Arthur Miller

When he marries her, Quentin is taking total responsibility for her. But, as he then discovers, she is irrevocably set on a course which can only end in self-destruction and in putting Quentin into a position of godlike responsibility for her life, she is also trying to pass over to him the responsibility for her death. To survive at all, he has to withdraw, to become a Separate Person.

In writing on this theme, Miller must have been at least partly aware of the danger that an audience would see the play as a play about his much publicized marriage with Marilyn Monroe. 'Maggie,' he wrote in *Life* after the play had opened 'is not in fact Marilyn Monroe. Maggie is a character in a play about the human animal's unwillingness or inability to discover in himself the seeds of his own destruction. Maggie is in this play because she most perfectly exemplifies the self-destructiveness which finally comes when one views oneself as pure victim. And she most perfectly exemplifies this view because she comes so close to being a pure victim – of parents, of a Puritanical sexual code and of her exploitation as an entertainer.'* Had he centred the play squarely on the Maggie relationship, though, it could hardly have been in greater danger of being taken autobiographically, and it might have been a far better play. As it is, Miller takes on far too much in attempting not only to link Quentin's failure over Maggie with all his other failures in human relationships, but to link his loss of innocence with the guilt of a whole civilization. The play cannot validate the equation it proposes between a Separate Person and a Person who Condones Concentration Camps. It is one thing to show how Quentin arrives at this equation inside his mind; it is quite another to imply, as Miller does, that it is generally valid.

Inside the world of Quentin's mind, his betrayal of Maggie (if it is a betrayal) gets linked with all the other betrayals. His mother has betrayed his father by becoming a Separate Person when he lost his money in the depression and she has betrayed Quentin when he was a small boy by practising a deception on him which made him feel abandoned. It does not become altogether clear from the play, but Miller has pointed out* that what Quentin saw of his parents' marriage causes him to fight too hard to stop his first wife, Louise, from

* This is quoted by Sheila Huftel in her book *Arthur Miller: The Burning Glass*. W. H. Allen (1966).

becoming a separate person. 'To wipe out his parents' separation, he wanted to run the train backwards, to make it not have happened.' He tries hard not to betray her with other women but in trying to stop himself from thinking of her as a separate person, he has unwittingly denied her her rights and created a huge overdraft of bitterness.

The relationship with Holga, who becomes his third wife, gets cemented after she has taken him to visit a concentration camp. Unlike the other women in his life, she is too realistic to have complete confidence in anyone's good faith and she believes that no one who survived the camps can possibly be wholly innocent.

No one they didn't kill can be innocent again.

But this attitude of hers is insufficiently dramatized and her whole character is insufficiently developed to take the enormous strain – which falls almost entirely on it – of linking the theme of personal betrayal with the theme of the concentration camps.

As Hannah Arendt has argued, the Jews may have been partly accomplices in their own slaughter by failing to resist. Similarly, Maggie is shown to co-operate with the people who are exploiting her in a way which will help to cause her destruction. But this too is an inadequate link between the two parts of the play.

Quite apart from the failure to give objective validity to Quentin's subjective equations, the monodrama method is a very dangerous one, as Miller was well aware. Writing about *Death of a Salesman*, he had said* that the way of telling the tale was as mad as Willy and that the form could not be grafted on to a character whose psychology it did not reflect.

> I have not used it since because it would be false to a more integrated – or less disintegrating – personality to pretend that the past and the present are so openly and vocally intertwined in his mind.

Far from disintegrating, Quentin is meant to be seen in the process of achieving a saner, if saddening, adjustment to reality.

The progress he makes during the play is very much like that which

* In his Introduction to the *Collected Plays*.

Arthur Miller

might be made during a successful course of psycho-analysis. The Listener is like an invisible analyst-figure seated in the auditorium just beyond the edge of the stage.

> QUENTIN: Hello! God, it's good to see you again! I'm very well. I hope it wasn't too inconvenient on such short notice. Fine I just wanted to say hello, really. Thanks. [*He sits on invitation. Slight pause.*] Actually, I called you on the spur of the moment this morning; I have a bit of a decision to make. You know – you mull around about something for months and all of a sudden there it is and you don't know what to do.

In using this device, Miller is insufficiently wary about the dangers of forcing the audience into an analyst role. Without doing anything to make Quentin interesting, he lets him button-hole the audience and pour out his confessions as if wanting to be judged. He is a lawyer who says he has become aware of looking at his life like a case, a series of proofs.

> When you're young you prove how brave you are, or smart; then, what a good lover; then a good father; finally, how wise, or powerful or what-the-hell-ever. But underlying it all I see now, there was a presumption. That I was moving on an upward path toward some elevation, where – God knows what – I would be justified, or even condemned – a verdict anyway. I think now that my disaster really began when I looked up one day – and the bench was empty. No judge in sight. And all that remained was the endless argument with oneself – this pointless litigation of existence before an empty bench.

On one level, the play is the case that Quentin pleads in his own defence after accusing himself of being an accomplice in Maggie's self-destruction. The defence rests partly on the argument that we are all accomplices – an argument it would be fairly easy to justify. But much of the narrative proceeds like a patient free-associating in an analyst's consulting room. Particularly at the beginning of the play, the transitions between one point and another are jerky and arbitrary, mimicking the movement of ideas and memories and conversations as they jostle for attention inside the brain. We move abruptly from Felice, a dancer who has offered Quentin her love without ever engaging his interest, to his mother's death, which introduces a brief examination of the difference between the attitudes of Quentin and his brother towards their father – a theme to which Miller will return in *The Price*. In writing of each memory as it crowds into Quentin's mind, Miller is trying to sidestep the necessity of building up to each episode, to consolidate its reality and to explain whatever needs to be explained in order to get the audience interested in what is going on.

Without preparation or development, isolated fragments of experience are liable to come over as melodramatic. We meet Quentin's father in a moment of Willy Loman-like euphoria, recovering from an operation in a hospital:

> Tell her to get some ice. When Mother comes you'll all have a drink! I got a bottle of rye in the closet. [*To* QUENTIN.] I tell you, kid, I'm going to be young. Mother's right; just because I got old I don't have to act old. I mean we could go to Florida, we could —

And his high spirits are immediately dashed when Quentin tells him that Mother died suddenly of a heart attack.

The scene about the difference between Holga's and Quentin's reactions to the concentration camp fails for the same reason: there is no build-up to it and we are not sufficiently involved in either of them for the dialogue to work in the way it is designed to. Like so much in the play, it gives the impression of drawing too directly on personal experience without trying hard enough to recreate it in a form that can carry its emotional impact forward to the audience. Any attempt to dramatize a stream of consciousness is bound to be a compromise because consciousness selects memories and impressions very quickly and very undramatically. A play needs to select and organize its material quite differently. In some ways the play is reminiscent of a novel by Virginia Woolf: the writing might have succeeded better if it had been either more subjective or more objective but the attempt to get the best of both modes blurs the outlines around both people and incidents. In some scenes the outlines are far too clear for us to accept them as being filtered through Quentin's memory. As in *Death of a Salesman* in trying to merge a character's memory of the past with an objective presentation of the past, Miller

65

Arthur Miller

is too transparently making the memory into a precise recording apparatus.

The scenes with Lou, an ex-communist professor of Law, and Mickey, his friend who decides to denounce him to the Committee, are given a little more breathing space but the characters both suffer from the way in which they are taken up and put down. The sequence in which Mickey tells Lou that it is his intention 'to name names' is more dramatic than anything which has preceded it in the first half of Act One but the method of narrating through Quentin's consciousness prevents Miller from introducing enough data about either of them. We get the impression of being forced to eavesdrop on an intimate and crucial scene between people we do not know.

Some of the points are subtle and extremely interesting, as when Mickey hits back against the far more sympathetic Lou by suggesting that he has handed his moral responsibility over to his wife, Elsie, in much the same way that a conformist who co-operates with the Committee is handing his soul over to the government:

> LOU [*turning on him*]: There is only one truth here. You are terrified! They have bought your soul!
>
> ELSIE *appears upstage, listening.* LOUISE *enters, watches.*
>
> MICKEY [*angrily, but contained*]: And yours? Lou! Is it all yours, your soul?
>
> LOU [*beginning to show tears*]: How dare you speak of my —
>
> MICKEY [*quaking with anger*]: You've got to take it if you're going to dish it out, don't you? Have you really earned this high moral tone – this perfect integrity? I happened to remember when you came back from your trip to Russia; and I remember who made you throw your first version into my fireplace!
>
> LOU [*with a glance toward* ELSIE]: The idea!
>
> MICKEY: I saw you burn a true book and write another that told lies! Because she demanded it, because she terrified you, because she has taken your soul!
>
> LOU [*shaking his fist in the air*]: I condemn you!
>
> MICKEY: But from your conscience or from hers? Who is speaking to me, Lou?

But the scene is not grafted into the play's organism well enough for

66

it to communicate either its full dramatic force or its relevance to Quentin's case.

Quentin's relationship with Louise is also explored subtly, but again we feel that, without a build-up, we simply are not in a position to accept this intimate discussion of intimacy.

LOUISE [*it is something, but not enough*]: Well, you've got a child; I'm sure that worries you.

QUENTIN [*deeply hurt*]: Is that all?

LOUISE [*with intense reasonableness*]: Look, Quentin, you want a woman to provide an – atmosphere, in which there are never any issues, and you'll fly around in a constant bath of praise —

QUENTIN: Well, I wouldn't mind a little praise, what's wrong with praise?

LOUISE: Quentin, I am not a praise machine! I am not a blur and I am not your mother! I am a separate person!

QUENTIN [*staring at her, and what lies beyond her*]: I see that now.

LOUISE: It's no crime! Not if you're adult and grown-up!

QUENTIN [*quietly*]: I guess not. But it bewilders me. In fact, I got the same idea when I realized that Lou had gone from one of his former students to another and none would take him —

LOUISE: What's Lou got to do with it? I think it's admirable that you —

QUENTIN: Yes, but I am doing what you call an admirable thing because I can't bear to be – a separate person. I think so. I really don't want to be known as a Red lawyer; and I really don't want the newspapers to eat me alive; and if it came down to it Lou could defend himself. But when that decent, broken man who never wanted anything but the good of the world sits across my desk – I don't know how to say that my interests are no longer the same as his, and that if he doesn't change I consign him to hell because we are separate persons!

LOUISE: You are completely confused! Lou's case has nothing –

QUENTIN [*grasping for his thought*]: I am telling you my confusion! I think Mickey also became a separate person —

LOUISE: You're incredible!

QUENTIN: I think of my mother, I think she almost became —

LOUISE: Are you identifying *me* with —

QUENTIN: Louise, I am asking you to explain this to me

67

Arthur Miller

because this is when I go blind! When you've finally become
a separate person, what the hell is there?

LOUISE [*with a certain unsteady pride*]: Maturity.

QUENTIN: I don't know what that means.

LOUISE: It means that you know another person exists, Quentin.
I'm not in analysis for nothing.

QUENTIN [*questing*]: It's probably the symptom of a typical
case of some kind, but I swear, Louise, if you would just once,
of your own will, as right as you are – if you would come to me
and say that something, something important was your fault
and that you were sorry, it would help.

   *In her pride she is silent, in her refusal to be brought down
   again.*

Louise?

LOUISE: Good God! What an idiot! [*She exits.*]

QUENTIN: Louise . . .

Here Miller is not even consistent. Louise makes her exit from the
stage before she makes her exit from Quentin's consciousness.

None of the early shifts of convention or narrative style are as
blatant as the one we get when we come to Maggie. Both Louise and
Holga are dim figures in comparison and though the amount of space
given to Maggie is justified if Quentin is obsessed to that degree by
the memory of her, the question of whether he is yet ready for
marriage with Holga needs more careful treatment. But in the Maggie
scenes, more than anywhere else, the balance is coming down on the
side of objective and uninterrupted re-presentation of the past. The
only important departure from realism is in the telescoping of time.
From the scene in the park to the final fight over the pills, we get a
panoramic view of the whole relationship. In itself, this is very well
done, but it would be even better if Miller were not constantly having
to make adjustments to integrate this narrative into the rest of the
play.

QUENTIN: Maggie, I've sat beside you in darkened rooms for
days and weeks at a time, and my office looking high and low
for me —

MAGGIE: No, you lost patience with me.

QUENTIN [*after a slight pause*]: That's right, yes.

MAGGIE: So you lied, right?

QUENTIN: Yes, I lied. Every day. We are all separate people. I tried not to be, but finally one is – a separate person. I have to survive too, honey.

MAGGIE: So where you going to put me?

QUENTIN [*trying not to break*]: You discuss that with your doctor.

MAGGIE: But if you loved me . . .

QUENTIN: But how would you know, Maggie? Do you know any more who I am? Aside from my name? I'm all the evil in the world, aren't I? All the betrayal, the broken hopes, the murderous revenge?

Admirable though it is to look for a continuity between private cruelties and public atrocities, these equations are far too facile. And in any case, by narrowing his focus to the marital relationship, Miller might have been able to find far subtler ways of making the same points, without referring so baldly to the camps.

As it is, he puts his language under a strain which it cannot take.

QUENTIN: But love, is love enough? What love, what wave of pity will ever reach this knowledge – I know how to kill? . . . I know, I know – she was doomed in any case, but will that cure? Or is it possible [*He turns toward the tower, moves toward it as toward a terrible God*] that this is not bizarre . . . to anyone? And I am not alone, and no man lives who would not rather be the sole survivor of this place than all its finest victims! What is the cure? Who can be innocent again on this mountain of skulls? I tell you what I know! My brothers died here [*He looks from the tower down at the fallen Maggie*] but my brothers built this place; our hearts have cut these stones! And what's the cure? . . . No, not love; I loved them all, all! And gave them willing to failure and to death that I might live, as they gave me and gave each other, with a word, a look, a trick a truth, a lie – and all in love!

HOLGA: Hello!

QUENTIN: But what will defend her? [*He cries up to* HOLGA]. That woman hopes!

She stands unperturbed, resolute, aware of his pain and her own.

Or is that [*struck, to the Listener*] exactly why she hopes, because she knows? What burning cities taught her and the

Arthur Miller

death of love taught me: that we are very dangerous! [*Staring, seeing his vision.*] And that, that's why I wake each morning like a boy – even now! I swear to you, I could love the world again! Is the knowing all? To know, and even happily, that we meet unblessed; not in some garden of wax after many, many deaths. Is the knowing all? And the wish to kill is never killed, but with some gift of courage one may look into its face when it appears, and with a stroke of love – as to an idiot in the house – forgive it; again and again . . . forever?

The emotionality of this is like a barage balloon that has come loose from its moorings. It is of no value in Quentin's defence of his position because it is not anchored to a specific context.

Had he not tackled such a great subject in such explicit terms, Miller's achievement might have been greater.

INCIDENT AT VICHY

Incident at Vichy was produced in New York later the same year. It is a more limited play but more successful within its limits. It is formally conventional but neatly structured, static but theatrical.

It takes up many of the same themes as *After the Fall*. Centring on a Nazi round-up of Jews in occupied France, it ventilates the questions of the extent to which the passive victims were accomplices in their own deaths and the degree of guilt in the survivors, both Jewish and non-Jewish.

The painter, Lebeau, and the actor, Monceau, refuse to help the psychiatrist Leduc make even an attempt at escape. All the evidence points to the Germans' intention of exterminating them but they are too scared of physical violence to face the facts.

> But what good are dead Jews to them? They want free labour. It's senseless. You can say whatever you like, but the Germans are not illogical; there's no conceivable advantage for them in such a thing.

The Major, who is not in the S.S. but is under orders to supervise the investigation of the suspects, is intelligent enough to understand the absurdity of what is happening and decent enough to feel deeply embarrassed about it. But he cannot save the lives of any of the prisoners except by sacrificing his own, and though Leduc tries to make him think that he ought to, the Major wins the argument by making Leduc admit that, given the chance, he would himself gladly walk out and leave the others to die.

Miller's novel *Focus* (1945) is about a non-Jew who looks Jewish and suffers so much at the hands of local anti-Semites that he ends up fighting with a Jew against them and leaving the policeman's assumption that he is Jewish unchallenged. In *Incident at Vichy*, an Austrian prince, Von Berg, who has been arrested by mistake, ends up by giving Leduc his pass to freedom and staying in his place in the detention room because he cannot feel or argue as the Major does.

When Leduc tells the prince that he has never analysed a gentile

Arthur Miller

who did not nurse a hidden dislike or hatred for the Jews, Von Berg is obviously genuine in thinking himself an exception:

> LEDUC [*standing, coming to him, a wild pity in his voice*]: Until you know it is true of you you will destroy whatever truth can come of this atrocity. Part of knowing who we are is knowing we are not someone else. And Jew is only the name we give to that stranger, that agony we cannot feel, that death we look at like a cold abstraction. Each man has his Jew; it is the other. And the Jews have their Jews. And now, now above all, you must see that you have yours – the man whose death leaves you relieved that you are not him, despite your decency. And that is why there is nothing and will be nothing – until you face your own complicity with this . . . your own humanity.
>
> VON BERG: I deny that. I deny that absolutely. I have never in my life said a word against your people. Is that your implication? That I have something to do with this monstrousness! I have put a pistol to my head! To my head!

But Leduc is easily able to demonstrate to him that he has connived at the persecution. He has remained friendly towards his Nazi cousin.

> It's not your guilt I want, it's your responsibility – that might have helped. Yes, if you had understood that Baron Kessler was in part, in some part, in some small and frightful part – doing your will. You might have done something then, with your standing, and your name and your decency, aside from shooting yourself!

It is this which induces Von Berg to take the risk of sacrificing his own life in order to save Leduc's.

But though this is a heroic action, Von Berg is hardly built up as a hero. Leduc has been more active in the play and he is the only character we come to know at all deeply. Von Berg we know only through his conversation and this detracts from the effectiveness and even from the plausibility of his final gesture. The actor is not given enough material to establish him as the sort of man who would behave in this way.

As usual, when he has a group of characters to establish, Miller is very adroit at bringing them separately to life. But, as he said in the interview* they all act severely within the limitations of their types, and, persuasive though it is, the dialogue does very little to make them into individuals in a specific historical context. There is very little, for instance, about the French attitude to the Germans. The generalization of the situation is deliberate, of course. The guilt of the decent German soldier, the French and the Jews themselves is presented as part of the universal guilt from which the only escape is in self-sacrifice. The Major's argument with Leduc shows that honourable behaviour is old fashioned:

MAJOR [*with a manic amusement, yet deeply questioning*]: Why do you deserve to live more than I do?

LEDUC: Because I am not capable of doing what you are doing. I am better for the world than you.

MAJOR: It means nothing to you that I have feelings about this?

LEDUC: Nothing whatever, unless you get us out of here.

MAJOR: And then what? Then what?

LEDUC: I will remember a decent German, an honourable German.

MAJOR: Will that make a difference?

LEDUC: I will love you as long as I live. Will anyone do that now?

MAJOR: That means so much to you – that someone love you?

LEDUC: That I be worthy of someone's love, yes. And respect.

MAJOR: It's amazing; you don't understand anything. Nothing of that kind is left, don't you understand that yet?

LEDUC: It is left in me.

MAJOR [*more loudly, a fury rising in him*]: There are no persons any more, don't you see that? There will never be persons again. What do I care if you love me?

We are all Separate Persons now. The French police are working with the Nazis and if any of the Jews escaped, the French citizens would hand them over to the police. And Von Berg's aristocratic friends have proved themselves equally terrorizable, equally conformist. When he talked to them about the slaughter of his Jewish musicians, they did not dare to react. Just as in *Focus* and in *The Crucible*, Miller is arraigning a conformist society in which everyone is drawn

* See page 14.

Arthur Miller

into the witch hunt. But here, instead of showing how the rot spreads, he takes it for granted and concentrates on a plot in which the argument and the action do not always work quite hand in hand. The points are made through the conversations; the suspense is created through what happens. One by one the prisoners are taken into a room to be examined and, apart from Von Berg, only one comes back. It is like watching Agatha Christie's *Ten Little Nigger Boys* without having any of the killing done on stage and without being in any doubt about who the murderers are.

THE PRICE

The phrase 'conversation piece' which had cropped up in several critical reactions to *Incident at Vichy*, recurred in reviews of *The Price*, but the play does not deserve it in anything like the same way. Though there is even less physical action than there is in *Incident at Vichy*, the new play is less open than its predecessor to the charge of divorcing the points made through argument from the points made through action.

The relationships between the four protagonists are constantly and dramatically shifting, and the arguments not only affect these shifts but are themselves subject to shifts. In *Incident at Vichy*, the discussions each went on in a straight line until they reached their main point; the discussions in *The Price* are liable to interruptions which either postpone their resolution or push it on to a different level. The conversation, in other words, is geared not so much to the pursuit of ideas as to the exploration of the characters and the kind of lives they have lived.

Miller had scarcely given himself space in any play since *The Crucible* to treat more than a single relationship in any depth. Here the economy of limiting himself to four characters pays off very well. Not only do Victor, the policeman, and his wife, Esther, arrive at a new understanding of each other but though this is the only confrontation he has had with him for years, there is substantial development in his relationship with his brother, Walter, a successful surgeon who once refused him the five hundred dollar loan he needed to make a start at university. And though Victor tries hard to avoid making any kind of personal contact with Solomon, the eighty-nine year-old antique dealer who arrives to offer him a price for the furniture in his father's flat, the canny old man manages to establish a relationship in which they both open out to each other.

Against the background of stacked furniture, the consummately managed opening conversation between Victor and Esther evokes their present and their past together. The mature flavour of the mixture of affection and rancour in their relationship makes us believe in them as a married couple. The argument they have now is obviously like so many arguments they have had before. The opportunist Esther must always have resented Victor's plodding straightforwardness and his stubborn idealism. The way she needs to keep going out for a drink shows the exact state of the balance between her tolerance and the strain he has put on it.

But though the present has grown discernibly out of the past, the past is not introduced in the way that it was in *All My Sons*. Here it is not primarily a matter of retelling incidents. Present and past are far more closely intertwined. Victor would not still be a humble policeman had he not preferred to take on the burden of supporting his father, who went broke in the Depression, rather than carve a selfish scientific career for himself, as he could have, like his brother. But now that he could retire from the police force, we see him making exactly the same kind of decision he has always made, ruled partly by moral scruple, partly by cautiousness, partly by generosity, partly by a deep-seated need to preserve the status quo. When Walter arrives, Victor has the chance of making twelve thousand dollars for himself out of selling the furniture if he collaborates in a tax-evading scheme, and he could land himself a well-paid semi-scientific job which is Walter's to dispose of. But he winds up with eleven hundred and fifty dollars for the furniture and staying in the police force.

The action is contrived, though, not merely to provide the characters with crossroads of decision like this. It is richly inlaid with specific details which furnish valuable pointers to the present texture of the life they lead. Esther's drinking, Victor's nocturnal teeth-grinding and the camel-hair coat Walter has been given by a patient from whom he removed two gallstones are examples of the details Miller fits aptly and effortlessly into the dialogue. Another is the nursing homes which Walter owned until he sold them after his breakdown:

> There's big money in the aged, you know. Helpless, desperate children trying to dump their parents – nothing like it.

This is typical of Miller's multiple use of detail: it helps to characterize Walter, it relates to the main theme of Victor's contrasting attitude to his old father and it provides a background to the breakdown. The reformed Walter is different, though not so different as he thinks he is.

> Fifty per cent of my time now is in City hospitals. And I tell you, I'm alive. For the first time. I do medicine, and that's it. [*Attempting an intimate grin.*] Not that I don't soak the rich occasionally, but only enough to live, really.

Miller's major triumph in the play is with Solomon, who is quite his best comic creation so far. The sequence in which Victor tries to make him name his price for the furniture is sustained delightfully for about half an hour. Each time that it comes to seem impossible that the delay can be protracted any longer, a new and enjoyable twist is contrived. The more the old man promises to come directly to the point, the more he beats about the bush. The more Victor rebuffs his friendliness, the more resiliently he bounces back.

> SOLOMON [*glancing off, he turns back to Victor with a deeply concerned look*]: Tell me, what's with crime now? It's up, hey?
> VICTOR: Yeah, it's up, it's up. Look, Mr Solomon, let me make one thing clear, heh? I'm not sociable.
> SOLOMON: You're not.
> VICTOR: No, I'm not; I'm not a businessman, I'm not good at conversations. So let's get to a price, and finish. Okay?
> SOLOMON: You don't want we should be buddies.
> VICTOR: That's exactly it.
> SOLOMON: So we wouldn't be buddies! [*He sighs.*] But just so you'll know me a little better – I'm going to show you something. [*He takes out a leather folder which he flips open and hands to Victor.*] There's my discharge from the British Navy. You see? 'His Majesty's Service.'

Despite himself, Victor is drawn into a conversation about what he was doing in the British Navy, about his age and at his next demonstration of impatience, it is Solomon's turn to get angry. He accuses Victor of not trusting him and starts to walk out without making an offer. Victor has to persuade him to stay. And it now emerges that like Victor, Solomon is at the crossroads of a decision – not about whether to retire but whether to go back into business.

This is not the only way in which Miller exploits the dramatic potential of Solomon's age. He uses it to put a perspective on the

Arthur Miller

furniture which is both funny and absolutely central to the play's subject.

> SOLOMON: You see, it's also this particular furniture – the average person he'll take one look, it'll make him very nervous.
>
> VICTOR: Solomon, you're starting again.
>
> SOLOMON: I'm not bargaining with you!
>
> VICTOR: Why'll it make him nervous?
>
> SOLOMON: Because he knows it's never gonna break.
>
> VICTOR [*not in bad humour, but clinging to his senses*]: Oh come on, will you? Have a little mercy.
>
> SOLOMON: My boy, you don't know the psychology! If it wouldn't break there is no more possibilities. For instance, you take [*crosses to table*] this table.... Listen! [*He bangs the table*]. You can't move it. A man sits down to such a table he knows not only he's married, he's got to stay married – there's no more possibilities. You're laughing, I'm telling you the factual situation. What is the key word today? Disposable. The more you can throw it away the more it's beautiful. The car, the furniture, the wife, the children – everything has to be disposable. Because you see the main thing today is – shopping. Years ago a person, he was unhappy, didn't know what to do with himself – he'd go to church, start a revolution – *something*. Today you're unhappy? Can't figure it out? What's the salvation? Go shopping.
>
> VICTOR [*laughing*]: You're terrific, I have to give you credit.
>
> SOLOMON: I'm telling you the truth! If they would close the stores for six months in this country there would be from coast to coast a regular massacre. With this kind of furniture the shopping is over, it's finished, there's no more possibilities, you *got* it, you see? So you got a problem here.

Which is followed immediately by the funniest of all the diversions, when Solomon produces a boiled egg from his briefcase, asking Victor whether he has any salt.

Incident at Vichy was a conversation piece in the sense that furniture, like most of the other issues, was introduced only in conversation: Lebeau explains that the reason he is still in the country is that his mother could not bear to sail for America and leave the furniture behind. In *The Price*, the furniture is physically present on stage and

Miller goes on finding new ways of excavating its dramatic mineral wealth, not just by using it as a base for dialogue but as a source for visual augmentation of the dialogue. If he does not altogether succeed in integrating the past in terms of action which fully exploits the medium, he at least comes much closer to doing so. Victor finds an old fencing foil which starts him testing his ageing body cn lunges. When Walter comes in, the furniture starts him reminiscing and Solomon keeps interrupting, offering to exclude this or that piece from the price he has agreed with Victor. One dress they find in the wardrobe is the dress their mother wore to Walter's wedding. Another strikes him as something his daughter, a designer might remake. Far from being a mere symbol of the past, the dusty contents of the room are made into a means of illuminating the present.

When Esther comes back, the discussion about the price serves to bring their conflicting loyalties and attitudes to the surface. Victor feels committed by what he has agreed with the old dealer, Esther is only concerned to get as much money as possible, Walter's main concern is to expiate the guilt he feels about having left Victor to be a failure while he became a success. Esther is all in favour of the tax-evading scheme and the job, but Victor is realistic enough to see that his brother is trying to buy him and he refuses to be bought because he has already paid – with the life he has had to live – for whatever quality it is in him that Walter envies.

There is a telling irony in the moments when Walter seems to approve of Victor's attitude more than Esther does. Her ineffective attempts to make Victor accept what Walter is offering are dramatically most effective. We see how much better this scene is, written as a triangular one, than it could possibly have been if the brothers had been alone together.

Solomon is made to have a giddy turn and Walter, in his medical capacity, looks after him, which gets the old man out of the room for this confrontation, but he keeps returning amusingly to interrupt. Each interruption, though, has a dramatic value which is not limited to its value as comic relief.

Walter's confessional speeches are quite acceptable because, unlike their counterparts in *After the Fall*, they have been led up to.

(They were not acceptable in performance and watching the play I

Arthur Miller

thought the writing was at fault; reading it I found it was the direction and the acting. The production we saw in London was the New York production with Albert Salmi, who took over from Pat Hingle as Victor, and Shepherd Strudwick, who took over from Arthur Kennedy, as Walter. Miller had himself taken over the direction when the play was on the road prior to the New York opening, because of a recasting crisis. Shepherd Strudwick was weak and Miller's direction made him worse. The monologue about the breakdown became a set piece, the subsequent narrative was glib and failed to take advantage of the build-up and in the final scenes, which call for speed and underplaying, Miller let Salmi and Strudwick go hammer and tongs at each other, shouting and overpointing all the climaxes right up to Walter's exit.)

In the writing, though, Miller interrelates his themes very deftly indeed: in talking about his breakdown, Walter is also talking about his guilt over his treatment of Victor. We have already heard, in Victor's first conversation with Esther, how Walter would not come to the telephone to speak to his brother. Now we understand why, but each of Walter's confessional speeches needs to be played very delicately in relation to the whole pattern of the past.

It looks for a moment as if the play is going off the rails when the subject of the father is introduced – a dead man who can only be integral to the plot, not the action. And there is a genuine weakness here. It is a key point in the plot that the selfish old father failed to relay to Victor a telephone offer from Walter to lend the vital five hundred dollars. But Miller does not make the mistake of putting all the responsibility for what has happened since on the dead man's shoulders. In a well phased climax, he reveals that the five hundred dollars were not, after all, the crux of the matter. They could not have been when the furniture was there, which, even then, would have fetched that amount of money. It looks as though we have reached the main climax when Walter reveals that the old man had money of his own but it is capped when Victor is forced to reveal that he knew all the time. And again Esther is very well used in the revelation.

> ESTHER: I want to understand what you're saying! You knew he had money left?

VICTOR: Not four thousand dol—

ESTHER: But enough to make out?

VICTOR [*crying out in anger and for release*]: I couldn't nail him to the wall, could I? He said he had nothing!

ESTHER [*stating and asking*]: But you knew better.

VICTOR: I don't know what I knew! [*He has called this out, and his voice and words surprise him. He sits staring, cornered by what he senses in himself.*]

ESTHER: It's a farce. It's all a goddamned farce!

VICTOR: Don't. Don't say that.

ESTHER: Farce! To stick us into a furnished room so you could send him part of your pay? Even after we were married, to go on sending him money? Put off having children, live like mice – and all the time you knew he . . . ? Victor, I'm trying to understand you. Victor? – Victor.

VICTOR [*roaring out, agonized*]: Stop it! Silence. [*Then*]: Jesus, you can't leave everything out like this. The man was a beaten dog, ashamed to walk in the street, how do you demand his last buck —?

What Victor is saying, in effect, is that he could not bear to be a Separate Person towards his father – the more so because, as he goes on to say, his mother acted like a Separate Person.

He couldn't believe in anybody any more, and it was unbearable to me! [*The unlooked-for return of his old feelings seems to anger him. Of* WALTER.] He'd kick him in the face; my mother [*he glances towards* WALTER *as he speaks; there is hardly a pause*] the night he told us he was bankrupt, my mother . . . It was right on this couch. She was all dressed up – for some affair, I think. Her hair was piled up, and long ear-rings? And he had his tuxedo on . . . and made us all sit down; and he told us it was all gone. And she vomited. [*Slight pause. His horror and pity twist in his voice.*] All over his arms. His hands. Just kept on vomiting, like thirty-five years coming up. And he sat there. Stinking like a sewer. And a look came on to his face. I'd never seen a man look like that. He was sitting there, letting it dry on his hands. [*Pause. He turns to* ESTHER.] What's the difference what you know? Do *you* do everything you know?

She avoids his eyes, his mourning shared.

Not that I excuse it; it was idiotic, nobody has to tell me that.

Arthur Miller

But you're brought up to believe in one another, you're filled full of that crap – you can't help trying to keep it going, that's all.

To some extent he is a victim, like Biff, but he is also responsible for his own fate.

There is so much to be said about *The Price* that it seems to me absurd that critics like Kenneth Tynan and Robert Brustein should think it worth spending time on its failure to refer to current political events. Interviewing Miller on television,* Tynan questioned him about this and he replied, rightly, that a play written in reference to current events is likely to be superficial and will be out of date as soon as the events are no longer topical.

Robert Brustein complained: 'How can a new play fail to be affected, if only indirectly, by the events of its time? ... Even conflicts within the family are inevitably informed by the frustrations that are driving the country mad.' As Miller said in his production note:

> As the world now operates, the qualities of both brothers are necessary to it; surely their respective psychologies and moral values conflict at the heart of the social dilemma.

And the social dilemma cannot be separated from the political dilemma either in the United States or over here.

* On Release. BBC 2. 1st March 1969.